Dragons Dogma II

Guide And Walkthrough

Tips And Tricks

Catalog

- Introduction 4
  - Dragon's Dogma 2: Guide content 4
  - Dragons Dogma 2: Tips and tricks 5
  - Dragons Dogma 2: basics 5
  - Dragons Dogma 2: FAQ 6
  - Dragons Dogma 2: List of all bosses 7
  - Dragons Dogma 2: Game length 7
  - Dragons Dogma 2: Trophies, Achievements 8
  - Dragons Dogma 2: Game editions 8
  - Dragons Dogma 2: System requirements 8
- basic 8
  - Interactive map 8
  - Shops 9
  - Inns 9
  - Riftstones 9
  - Seekers Tokens 10
  - Golden Trove beetles 10
  - Oracles 10
  - barberies 10
  - Portcrystals 11
  - Campsite 11
  - Chest 11
  - Tips and tricks 11
  - be careful when using Load from last Inn Rest 12
  - Remember that ingredients in your inventory go bad 12
  - Rest in inns often 13
  - Use elements of the environment during combat 13
  - Grapples break through opponent's defense 13
  - Always have a full team 14
  - Pay attention to the weight of carried items 14
  - Check every exclamation mark on the map 15
  - buy new skills 15
  - Use keyboard shortcuts, commands and items 16
  - Character creator 16
  - how to use the character creator? 17
  - how to change appearance? 17
  - Does the choice of race affect anything? 18

What does height affect?	18
What does weight affect?	18
What is Moniker?	19
All vocations, classes	19
basic starting vocations	19
Advanced vacations	20
hybrid vacations	21
Pawns	21
Who are Pawns?	22
how to get Pawns?	22
best vocation for Pawn	23
best specialization for Pawn	23
bestiary, all bosses	23
Skeletons	24
Specters	24
Saurians	24
Chopper	25
Cyclops	25
Ogre	25
Minotaur	26
Griffin	26
Chimera	27
Drake	27
Dullahan	27
Golem	27
hobgoblins	28
Knacker	28
Rattlers	28
Slimes	28
Talos	28
Undead	29
Wight	29
All Portcrystals locations	29
Portcrystal in vernworth (fixed)	29
Portcrystal in harve village (fixed)	30
Portcrystal for completing Feast of Deception	30
Portcrystal for solving Sphinx's puzzles	30
Portcrystal for completing Trial of Archery	30
Portcrystal in the Griffin's nest	31

- Portcrystal bought from The Dragonforged 31
- FAQ 31
  - Important Choices 31
    - Go to the capital with Gregor or alone? 31
    - Should I give gold to Sven? 33
    - Let the spy go or not? 34
    - Should I reveal the beggar's secret? 36
  - vocations 37
    - how to change vocation? 38
    - how to unlock Mystic Spearhand? 39
    - how to unlock Mystic Spearhand? 40
    - how to unlock Warrior and Sorcerer vocations? 40
    - how to complete the "vocation Frustration" quest? 40
  - Quest 41
    - Do quests have a time limit? 41
    - Where to find Fruit Roborant for the little girl in Melve? 42
    - Where is the room with books? 43
    - how to steal the queen's letter? 45
    - how to complete Disa's Plot quest? 46
    - how to buy a house? 47
    - how to solve the Sphinx's riddles? 48
    - What to do before the coronation? 53
    - Point of no return 53
  - Romances 54
    - Are there romances? 54
    - how to romance Ulrika? 55
    - how to romance Wilhelmina? 58
  - exploration 60
    - Is there an open world? 60
    - What do the exclamation marks on the mini-map mean? 61
    - how to increase carrying capacity? 62
    - Is there fast travel? 64
    - how to find the elf village? 66
  - Mechanics and Collectibles 67
    - Is there multiplayer? 67
    - Multiplayer in Dragons Dogma 2 68
    - how to cast spells? 68

how to save the game?..69
What are Wakestones used for?..71
What are the uses of Seeker Tokens?..72
Is there a day and night cycle?..73
What items can be safely sold?...75
Why does my maximum health decrease over time?.......................76
how to unlock Dwarven Smithing?...77
What is Dragonsplague?..80

Introduction

Dragon's Dogma 2 is an action role-playing game played from a third-person perspective. The player takes on the role of a character called the "Arisen", a hero marked by a dragon whom they must defeat. The player explores the world they live in, taking on quests, and fighting monsters, while being caught up in a geopolitical conflict between two kingdoms. To assist in this, the Arisen relies on allies called "Pawns", non-playable characters who join the player's party. These characters are AI-controlled, but function like player-controlled avatars, able to assist in fights, provide information on enemies, and give guidance to active quests. Players can each create and customize their avatar and their own Pawn character with different genders, appearances, and race. In addition, players can recruit two additional Pawns that have been created by other players.

Dragons Dogma 2 guide is the best beginner's guide, tips for character development and combat. We describe all mechanics, collectibles, maps, character creator and classes, difficulty levels, builds, bosses, system requirements, game length, controls.

Our guide to *Dragon's Dogma 2* will help you fully explore the game world and learn its mechanics. We have focused heavily on various secrets and collectibles, as well as on all the different bosses you will encounter in the game. You'll also find answers to frequently asked questions and information about **character classes (vocations)**, equipment, **fast travel**, character creator, and more. The whole thing concludes with a trophy guide, in which we explain how to get the platinum and complete the game 100%.

- Dragon's Dogma 2: Guide content
- Dragons Dogma 2: Tips and tricks
- Dragons Dogma 2: basics
- Dragons Dogma 2: FAQ

- Dragons Dogma 2: List of all bosses
- Dragons Dogma 2: Game length
- Dragons Dogma 2: Trophies, Achievements
- Dragons Dogma 2: Game editions
- Dragons Dogma 2: System requirements

Dragon's Dogma 2: Guide content

The first chapter of the guide primarily consists of **tips and tricks**, which will help you start your adventure with the game and avoid common mistakes. You will find out about, e.g. the available **character classes** and which vocation will be best for your playstyle. We also describe **the character creator**.

The next section, FAQ, is dedicated to answering the most important and frequently asked questions by players. here we explain, among other things, whether the game has a multiplayer mode, **fast travel**, and if side quests have **time limits**.

There is also room for collectibles and **bosses**, both story and optional. We explain how to deal with powerful opponents in hand-to-hand or long-range combat.

The guide ends with an appendix in which you will find information about **the game's length**, available languages, game editions, controls, **PC system requirements**, graphic modes on consoles, and, above all, **a trophy guide** in which we describe how to obtain all achievements/trophies in the game.

Dragons Dogma 2: Tips and Tricks

1. **be careful with the Load from Last Inn Rest option** - the rather enigmatic option to load the game in the last inn may overwrite your game progress. be careful when you use it.

2. **Remember that items rot in your inventory** - some delicate items such as fruit or meat will rot if you leave them in your inventory for too long. Regularly use up items that can expire.

3. **Rest often at inns** - a night spent at an inn saves your game and fully restores lost health and stamina.

4. **Take advantage of your surroundings during combat** - don't be afraid to use elements such as boulders or exploding barrels to gain an advantage over your opponent.

5. **Grapples break the defense of smaller enemies** - if a smaller enemy is protecting himself with a shield, you can try to grab him to break his block.

6. **Rent support Pawns on an ongoing basis** - Pawns rented from other players do not level up with you. Therefore, you will need to replace them on an ongoing basis.

7. **Balance the weight of your equipment** - excessive load will negatively affect your character's stamina. Continually get rid of unnecessary items.

8. **Check what is hidden under the exclamation marks** - the exclamation marks appearing on the map are points spotted by one of your Pawns. They are often interesting places or treasures.

9. **Buy new skills** - visit the Guild building from time to time to develop, modify or even completely change your vocation.

10. **Use keyboard shortcuts, commands and items** - the game does not communicate very well that there are useful keyboard shortcuts. Use them to issue commands to the party, as well as to quickly use items.

For more detailed information and useful tips, check out the appropriate page in our guide.

Dragons Dogma 2: basics

1. Character creator - in DD2 you will find an extremely extensive character creation system. On our website, we describe its most important mechanics and how certain aspects of the character can affect further gameplay.
2. All vocations (classes) - on this page you will find a list of all vocations available in the game along with descriptions that will help you choose the perfect class for you.
3. Pawns - on this page you will find a handful of the most important information about the Pawns system available in the game.
4. Locations of all Portcrystals - learn how to find all fast travel hubs in the game.

Dragons Dogma 2: FAQ

1. Is there multiplayer? - here, you will find out if you can play the game with friends.
2. Do quests have a time limit? - we explain how tasks and missions with a time limit work.
3. Is there an open world? - on this page, you will find out what you can expect from the world available in DD2.
4. how to cast spells? - a collection of basic information about the magic system available in the game.
5. how to save your progress? - is DD2 another soulslike without manual save? From this page, you'll learn how the game saving mechanics work.
6. What are Wakestones used for? - we explain how items thanks to which you can revive a dead character work.
7. What do the exclamation marks on the mini-map mean? - on this site, you will find out what the mysterious exclamation marks that appear on your mini-map from time to time mean.

8. how to unlock the Warrior and Sorcerer vocations? - instructions that will easily unlock you access to two advanced vocations.

9. Where to find Fruit Roborant for the girl in Melve? - we suggest how to find a special ingredient for one of the first side quests in the game.

10. how to increase a character's carrying capacity? - on this page, you will find advice on increasing the capabilities of your character in terms of how much equipment you can carry.

11. What are Seeker Tokens for? - we present the most important information related to this common collectible.

12. Is there a day and night cycle? - we advise on how to deal with the passing time in the game and traveling after sunset.

13. What items can be safely sold? - we suggest what and when to sell to free up some space in the inventory and earn some gold.

14. Is fast travel available in the game? - on this page we explain whether there is fast travel between points on the map.

15. **What is the level cap?** - from this site you will find out to what is the maximum level your character can have.

16. **how to die less often?** - in this place, you will find a number of tips on how to deal with opponents you encounter in the game world more efficiently.

17. Why does my maximum health decrease over time? - learn what the Loss effect is and how to get rid of it.

18. how to unlock Mystic Spearhand? - we suggest how to unlock the hybrid vocation fighting with a spear.

19. Go to the capital with Gregor or alone? - on this page you will find the answer to the question whether it is worth going to the capital with the captain, or maybe it is better to organize your own transport.

20. Should I give gold to Sven? - we explain whether it is worth helping the mysterious boy met on the streets of the capital.

21. Are there romances in the game? - we explain the NPC affinity system works.
22. How to find the room with books? - on this page, you will find the location of the room you have to find during the main story.
23. How to steal the queen's letter? - we suggest how to complete the stealth mission in the castle.
24. How to buy a house? - find out where and for how much you can buy your own house in DD2.
25. What is Dragonsplague? - we explain and warn about the mysterious curse haunting Pawns.
26. How to solve the Sphinx's riddles? - from this page, you will learn how to answer the tricky questions of the riddle master.
27. Let the spy go or not? - we present possible solutions to the problem of a spy tracking the Arisen.
28. Should I reveal the beggar's secret? - on this page, you will see possible solutions to an interesting side plot related to the mysterious beggar.

Dragons Dogma 2: List of all bosses

Dragons Dogma 2 **offers players fights with various opponents.** Among them will be creatures smaller and larger, less and more dangerous, fighting alone or in a group. More information about what monsters appear in the game and how to fight them can be found on a separate guide page.

Dragons Dogma 2: Game length

Completing *Dragons Dogma 2* will take you at least several dozen hours. You can read more about that on a separate page of the guide.

Dragons Dogma 2: Trophies, Achievements

On a separate page, you'll find a detailed trophy guide, which describes how to get the platinum trophy and thus complete the game 100%.

Dragons Dogma 2: Game editions

Dragons Dogma 2 was released in several editions differing in price and content. On a separate page of the guide, we described **all editions of the game**, as well as the bonuses received for purchasing the title in pre-order.

Dragons Dogma 2: System requirements

1. **Operating system:** Windows 10 (64-bit), Windows 11 (64-bit),
2. **Processor:** Intel Core i5 10600, AMD Ryzen 5 3600 or better,
3. **RAM:** 16 Gb,
4. **Graphics card:** nVIDIA GeForce GTX 1070, AMD Radeon RX 5500 XT with 8 Gb vRAM or better,
5. **Disk space:** 100 Gb (SSD),
6. **DirectX:** version 12.

More information about system requirements and **graphic modes on consoles** can be found on a separate page in our guide.

Basic

Interactive map

Dragons Dogma 2 map - all settlements, caves, Rifstones, campfires, Seekers Tokens, Portcrystals, caves and much more. Thanks to our map you'll finish the game on 100%.
Dragons Dogma 2 is a huge game with a world that can seem very overwhelming. **On this page of the guide you will find our interactive map, where we have marked places and objects that may be useful to you - settlements, caves, bonfires, Seekers Tokens and many others.**

- Shops
- Inns
- Riftstones
- Seekers Tokens
- Golden Trove beetles
- Oracles
- barberies
- Portcrystals
- Campsite
- Chest

Shops

1. There is no need to explain what a shop is - you can buy various items there and also sell loot and unnecessary things. Depending on the store, their

offer will be different, although it does not matter if you intend to sell - **each store will buy everything from you at the same price**.

2. **On our map you will find different types of shops**, such as Apothecaries (sells healing items), blacksmiths (sells weapons) and Armories (sells armor).

3.

Inns

1. At inns, you can rest after your hard journey, **fully regenerating your health and restoring your lost maximum health**.

2. **Paying for a rest at an inn will also save your game**, allowing you to go back to the last inn you visited if necessary.

Riftstones

1. **Riftstones scattered throughout the map are extremely important because they allow you to recruit new Pawns**. Many Riftstones are initially destroyed - interacting with them will repair and activate them, and reward you with a certain amount of Rift Crystals.

2. **Unlike recruiting Pawns we encounter on the road, Riftstones allows us to use special filters and thus find a Pawn that suits your preferences** - having the class, trait or skill you desire.

Seekers Tokens

1. **Seekers Tokens are scattered around the game world.** There are 220 of them in total.
2. **You can return the collected tokens at any Guild headquarters** - for returning specific numbers of tokens, you will receive rewards such as unique rings or armor.

Golden Trove beetles

1. **Gold beetles are found in specific locations in the game world, most often on trees and various stone walls.** They shine in gold, making them easier to spot.
2. **Consuming a beetle will increase the maximum carrying capacity of your hero or main Pawn by 0.15 kg** - so it is worth looking for them.

Oracles

1. **The Oracles, in exchange for a small monetary fee, will give you a hint about the quest** you have set as a priority.
2. The Oracle's hints may be more or less obvious - **they may prove useful if you don't know what to do next**.

Barberies

1. Barberies are special stores **where you can modify your appearance**.
2. **In exchange for a hefty fee, you can change your hairstyle or apply makeup**. You can also use a special item here to completely change the appearance of your hero or main Pawn.

Portcrystals

1. **Portcrystals are special places that are fast travel hubs**. To teleport to one of them, you have to activate it and use the Ferrystone item.
2. Two Portcrystals available in the game are stationary. The rest is portable and can be placed anywhere on the map. You will receive them for performing specific tasks or activities.

Campsite

1. Campsites are places scattered around the map where the party can **rest, regenerate, cook food, and modify their set of skills**.
2. To use the camp, **you must have a Camping kit**.

Chest

1. There are chests **filled with various treasures** scattered throughout the game map.
2. **The chests differ in appearance**. The wooden ones are common and usually contain more modest loot. Metal chests are harder to find, but often hide rare items such as new equipment.

Tips and Tricks

DD2 is a huge game that can easily overwhelm you with its size and number of mechanics. On this page, we'll give you a handful of start-up tips that will make your first hours with the title easier.

Dragons Dogma 2 is characterized by a large open world and a lot of various mechanics and activities. Such a lot to learn and master may cause dizziness for novice players, especially those who haven't had contact with the previous installments of the series. **That's why we have prepared on this website a set of the most important tips and tricks that will make your entry into the world of Capcom's new RPG much more enjoyable.**

- Be careful when using Load from last Inn Rest
- Remember that ingredients in your inventory go bad overtime
- Rest in inns often
- Use elements of the environment during combat
- Grapples break through opponent's defense
- Have a full team at all times

- Pay attention to the weight of carried items
- Check every exclamation mark on the map
- Buy new skills
- Use keyboard shortcuts, commands and items

Be careful when using Load from last Inn Rest

1. In the main menu and the game over screen, you can continue and return to the game by choosing the Load from Last Inn Rest option. Choosing this option is not recommended, **as it will revert your entire progress made after leaving the Inn**.

2. You may have problems distinguishing between Inns and campsites, as they work similarly - replenish health and stamina of the entire team and allow you to wait out until morning or dusk. It would seem that campsites are mobile inns. Unfortunately, they are not - **Load from Last Inn Rest option won't bring you back to the last campsite, but to the last inn, erasing your progress**. As a result, you shouldn't use this option, unless you have recently used an inn or are ready to replay a large chunk of the game.

3. **Still, this option has one advantage over a standard loading of a save state** - if you load your game at the death screen, your maximum health level will be lowered until your next visit to an inn or a campsite. Loading the inn save will allow you to continue the game with full health capacity.

If you want to learn more about the save system in DD2, visit how to save the game? page of our guide.

Remember that ingredients in your inventory go bad

1. In DD2, a quite interesting mechanic related to inventory items has been implemented. **Items such as fruit, meat or plants left in the bag of the Arisen or one of the Pawns for too long will begin to rot over time, losing their previous properties.** To avoid this, try to use up the leftover ingredients on an ongoing basis by creating potions, elixirs, or other products from them.
2. An alternative may also be **baking, drying or cooking food**, which should extend its edibility window. In cities, you will also come across special food containers that slow down the process of decay and rotting.

Rest in inns often

1. In every settlement, you will find an inn where, for a certain fee, you can spend the night and rest. **Staying at the inn saves the game and fully restores your health and stamina. Additionally, your maximum health is returned to its normal capacity** - injuries in combat gradually lower the maximum health value, which means the longer you delay a good rest, the weaker you become.
2. **bonfires found along routes between settlements work similarly, but they do not offer the option to save your progress.** To be able to save, you need camp kits that can be bought from merchants or found as loot. Resting with a camp kit is cheaper than staying at an inn, but these items are heavy to carry around. You also

need to eliminate every opponent found in the vicinity of the planned camp - otherwise, you risk an ambush.

3. **Ultimately, inns are a better choice than camp kits** - however, don't be afraid to use the latter if you need to rest and the next settlement is still far away.

Use elements of the environment during combat

1. Combat in *Dragons Dogma 2* is multi-faceted and gives the player a lot of freedom when it comes to damaging opponents. One of the things to keep in mind is using elements of the environment. **Skillful use of these objects may produce unusually good results**.

2. **For example, you can pick up boulders and explosive barrels and throw them at the opponent** - such moves are even more powerful if you play as a melee class like Fighter. You can also pick up enemies and throw them into chasms or terrain obstacles.

Grapples break through opponent's defense

1. **Many enemies in the game wield shields that offer them additional protection from your attacks**. To counter them, you can wait for the right moment, attack from behind, wait for one of your Pawns to knock the enemy down - or simply break his guard with a grapple, knocking him down or throwing him over your shoulder. With an enemy incapacitated, you can unleash a flurry of unblockable attacks or pick him up and throw him.

Always have a full team

1. Pawns are a core element of the game and their composition is one of the deciding factors in battles. In addition to the main pawn you created, you can also hire up to two support pawns. **To do this, you need to use a Riftstone** - one can be found in every settlement, and there are additional ones occasionally found along roads. After interacting with one, a comprehensive search engine will open, where you can filter available Pawns based on their vocation, race, level, and many other parameters.

2. **While exploring, you may also come across traveling pawns** - talking to them will allow you to hire them. Pawns also have unique traits that you should pay attention to - e.g. Logistician trait will make the pawn automatically craft items if he has the necessary ingredients in his inventory.

3. **Support pawns are slightly different from the main hero and main pawn**. First and foremost, they cannot gain experience, which means they will forever remain at the level at which you recruited them. Pawns at the same level as the main character can be recruited for free, but higher-level pawns require Rift Crystals, a special currency obtained through exploration. You can outfit support pawns with better equipment, but they will take it with them after dismissing them - if you play with online features, the equipment you've given the aide will be received by the player who created the pawn.

4. **Replacing support pawns with stronger ones at a regular basis is important and will make battles much easier.** Strive to make your team diverse in terms of classes, attitudes and specializations - this will make you more versatile.

Pay attention to the weight of carried items

1. The inventory system in *Dragons Dogma 2* may seem too complicated for a newcoming player. Unlike many other RPG games, the carrying capacity of characters is quite low, making your heroes unable to carry too many items. **The more overloaded you are, the faster your stamina runs out and the slower it regenerates, which can make both exploration and combat more difficult.**

2. There are several ways to manage load capacity. **having a full team is the most important of them - the more team members, the more backpacks to carry items, so make sure to distribute carried loot between pawns** to mitigate load so every hero can give his 100% in combat. Also, remember to sell unneeded items in settlements, and store old equipment in chests found in inns.

3. To increase carrying capacity, you can also consume Golden Trove beetles - occasionally found golden beetles. **each consumed beetle will increase the carrying capacity of the main character or the main pawn by 0.15 kg.**

Check every exclamation mark on the map

1. While exploring the world of *Dragons Dogma 2*, you will frequently encounter exclamation marks on the mini-map. **They appear when one of your pawns notices something that may be useful to you.**

2. various things can be hidden under exclamation marks - Seekers Tokens, chests, groups of enemies or notes hanging on the walls. **It is worth checking them out, as you may come across useful items.**

Buy new skills

1. **Leveling up your vocation unlocks new skills that will make you more powerful and more versatile.** however, the upgrades are not available right after ascending to a new level - you first need to buy them by spending Discipline Points received for defeating enemies. **Skills are bought in guild headquarters found in settlements.** If there is no guild headquarters in the given settlement, check out the inn.

2. **Skills are divided into three types. Weapon Skills are active skills that are cast with keyboard shortcuts** - you can equip up to four at a time. **Core Skills are abilities that are active permanently** after buying, expanding your repertoire. Augments are passive bonuses to stats e.g. improved defense - you can equip up to 6 at a time. **They also transfer between classes - purchased Augments can be used even after changing to another vocation.**

3. **Remember to regularly visit guild headquarters to buy new skills. They can, among others, provide new solutions for typical problems** - for example, Fighter's Airward Slash allows him to reach airborne enemies with his attacks, while Compass Slash helps when facing multiple opponents. **Purchased skills can be equipped and exchanged at inns and bonfires.**

Use keyboard shortcuts, commands and items

1. **One of the most important, yet unexplained mechanics** *of Dragons Dogma 2* **are the keyboard shortcuts, which appear right next to the mini-map.** They are

assigned to keys 1-4 on the keyboard and to the D-pad on the controller. **It is worth using them, as they can make the game much easier.**

2. **Shortcuts are for giving orders to your Pawns, influencing their behavior.** The command "**Go!**" will cause the Pawns to scatter on the battlefield or start interacting with nearby objects, such as crates. The command "**To me!**" makes the Pawns stay close to the main character during a fight or teleport closer if they have strayed too far. The command "**Wait!**" causes the Pawns to stop in place until another order is given, and during combat they stop attacking, supporting the main character in other ways. The command "**help!**" causes Pawns to focus on helping and healing the main character from wounds or status effects.

3. **holding the button responsible for Weapon Arts changes the operation of hotkeys - instead of orders, they switch to items.** You can quickly consume items that restore health, stamina, light or extinguish the oil lamp, or open the item menu without the need to navigate through the pause menu.

Character creator

The character creator in DD2 is extremely extensive and detailed. On this page of the guide we describe the wizard in depth, explain how to create a playable hero and main pawn, as well as which elements of the wizard affect gameplay.

The character creator in *Dragon's Dogma 2* is an extensive and complicated toy that allows the player to create their dream hero, even modifying such details as the thickness of the calves or the angle of bending the limbs at the elbows and knees. **Creating a character is straightforward and intuitive, but exploring all the features the creator offers can extend the process to several hours.** Some elements of the creator are not strictly cosmetic, having some impact on the gameplay. **On this page of our guide, we have described the most important functions of the character creator and what you should be aware of.**

- how to use the character creator?
- how to change appearance?
- Does the choice of race affect anything?
- What does height affect?
- What does weight affect?
- What is Moniker?

how to use the character creator?

1. **The character creator allows you to create both a playable character and your main pawn - an artificial intelligence-controlled companion who will keep up with you during your adventure.** The creation process is almost the same. **There are five slots in the creator for both our hero and pawn**, which means you can save up to ten characters.

2. **You can create your protagonist or pawn from scratch or based on a selected character already built into the game.** When presented with the first choice, you must select a basic body (male or female), race (human or cat-like beastren), and then customize the body from a variety of available options. next, you will create a basic head, choosing the face that suits you best.

3. **After creating or selecting a basic character, you can start editing the details.** You can modify, e.g. hair, facial features, body structure, height, limbs length. At the very end, you need to choose a character class, voice, name, and nickname. **When creating a pawn, you will also choose its attitude, which affects how it will behave during combat** - it will stay away from enemies, attack aggressively, or gather useful materials.

how to change appearance?

1. **You don't need to worry excessively about making mistakes - nearly every aspect of your characters can be altered after the game begins.** however, this requires a special item. The only exception is the race - **after making a choice in the creator and starting the game, the race can no longer be changed.**

2. **This means that you can change your character's class. We suggest that your main character and main pawn should be from different classes**, providing you with greater maneuverability during the game. We wrote more about the available classes on a separate guide page.

Does the choice of race affect anything?

1. **Since the character's race is the only element that cannot be changed after finishing the character creator, it can be assumed that it has some influence on the gameplay.** The page will be updated when we learn what differences result from choosing between a human and a beastren.

2. While you officially cannot create other popular fantasy races, **like elves or dwarves, the creator enables you to alter a human to look like such a race** - for instance, you can give your character pointed ears or abundant hair.

What does height affect?

1. One of the available sliders is the character's height - from 160 to 215 centimeters, regardless of race or body type. In the previous part of the series, **character height had a minor impact on the gameplay** - taller characters' attacks had a greater range, and shorter characters could pass between the legs of some larger opponents and pass through tight passages.
2. **At this point, it's unconfirmed whether the character's height affects the gameplay in** *Dragon's Dogma 2*. The page will be updated when we obtain more information.

What does weight affect?

1. **Almost all character modifications affect its final weight.** The further you move each slider to the right, the more the character's weight will increase.
2. **The character's carrying capacity increases as its weight grows, but the stamina regeneration speed decreases rapidly.** This means that classes such as warrior can gain more weight. The heavier your hero is supposed to be armored, the more they should weigh.

What is Moniker?

Moniker, or nickname, is **the special nickname of your Arisen or Pawn. It will be visible to other players when the actual name of your character is marked by the system as offensive or vulgar.** Playing solo, you will keep your name, and the nickname will only be visible to other players. You can choose a Moniker from a fairly long list of popular names and words.

All vocations, classes

DD2 offers players a choice among a dozen character classes, called vocations. On this page, we will introduce you to the characteristics of each of them, so you can choose the role that is perfect for you.

Dragons Dogma 2, similarly to the first installment of the series, **gives players access to a variety of vocations** that the world of the game, are equivalent to character classes known from other games. each vocation has a different area of expertise, **offering a variety of playstyles and different assumed roles in the team**. On this page of our guide, we provide a list of all possible vocations, explain what they focus on when it comes to combat, and finally show how to unlock more advanced classes.

- basic starting vocations
- Advanced vacations
- hybrid vacations

basic starting vocations

Starting vocations are the 4 basic hero archetypes to which you receive access at the very beginning of the game. You make the choice of the vocation in the character creation screen. each of these focus on a different aspect of combat and every player should find something for himself among them.

1. **Fighter** - a melee combatant **equipped with a sword and shield**. During clashes, Fighters bear the brunt of enemy attacks, protecting less durable team members. Among the abilities of this class, we have improving damage dealt to targets, increasing defense, or taunting enemies. **This class will appeal to players who prefer direct, close combat. This vocation can be chosen for your Pawns.**

1. **Archer** - a hero specializing in ranged combat, equipped with a bow. They make up their low survivability with nimbleness and agility **which allows them to quickly relocate and change positions in the course of combat**. The long effective range of a bow helps Archers hurt e.g. flying enemies. This archetype will work great as support for less mobile party members that fight in melee range. **This vocation can be chosen for your Pawns.**

1. **Thief** - this class **specializes in inflicting damage with fast combinations of surprise attacks**. While not as tough as shield-equipped Fighters, they make up their fragility with extended mobility. **Thieves will also be useful during battles against larger opponents, as this class can climb the creatures to reach more vulnerable areas of them.** The uniqueness of this class makes Thieves shine only when they complement a well-composed team. **This vocation can be chosen for your Pawns.**

1. **Mage** - a ranged spell caster. These students of mystic arts are perfect in supporting roles. **Access to a wide range of offensive and defensive spells allows them to both attack enemies and cast protective spells on allies.** healing spells will turn the tide of numerous battles. be careful, however, as **cloth-wearing mages won't survive long if they get into an effective range of enemies**. **This vocation can be chosen for your Pawns.**

Advanced vacations

These are variations of basic vocations. **You can unlock them through quests**, and each serves as an upgrade to the basic respective vocation, offering new skills and abilities.

1. **Warrior** - this class abandons the shield in favor of heavy two-handed weapons. The new weaponry allows them to deal even more damage. Unlike Fighters, the lack of a shield may mean increased susceptibility to enemy attacks, so skillful positioning on the battlefield will be very important. This vocation can be chosen for your Pawns.

1. **Sorcerer** - magic wielder **specializing in area of effect offensive spells.** The enhanced power of his spells **comes at a cost of more difficult and longer casting time**. This means that for a Sorcerer, correct positioning is even more important, as the casting process will be the time when they are the most vulnerable. The abilities of this class will be especially useful during long battles with bosses or large groups of enemies. **This vocation can be chosen for your Pawns.**

hybrid vacations

Archetypes combining elements of different classes. hybrids are interesting mixtures that **will appeal to players looking for less obvious solutions.** Like Advanced vocations, **these classes will also need to be unlocked first. It's worth noting that hybrid vocations are only available for player character.**

1. **Mystic Spearhand** - a class **combining melee combat and ranged spellcasting**. The versatile nature of the spear allows Spearhands to fight in different positions on the battlefield. **Class representatives also have access to special spells that help, for example, with crowd control.**

1. **Magick Archer** - an archer employing magic arrows. **Magic projectiles always hit their target, and can additionally be infused with power of elements.**

This ranged class will be perfect at locating and dealing damage to weak points of opponents.

1. **Trickster** - a very interesting type of hero **that utilizes smoke from incense burner and magic in combat.** Trickster will work best as a support hero, where his devious tricks will wreak mayhem on enemies while the caster remains at a safe distance. **A proficient player can, for example, force enemies to attack each other or summon illusions that will bring destruction to his opponents.** In addition to previously mentioned skills, **this class has also a choice of buffs that can be applied to his team members.**
1. **Warfarer** - a complex archetype combining elements of many other vocations. by choosing it, **you will be able to utilize skills and tools available to other classes.** This class provides immense flexibility when it comes to choosing your preferred playstyle, but getting the best out of it will require planning and dedication.

Pawns

In DD2 the well-known system of pawns - loyal companions of the Arisen - returns. On this page we will introduce you to how this system works.

Pawns are the companions of the controlled hero in *Dragons Dogma 2*. **Their purpose is to support you in combat, and sometimes also help during exploration.** As the gameplay and characters develop, Pawns will become invaluable members of your team. On this page, we provide an introduction to the topic of Pawns, show what roles in the team they can play, and finally what types of interactions may ensue between the player and his ally.

- Who are Pawns?
- how to get Pawns?

- Pawns - best vocations
- best specialization for Pawn

Who are Pawns?

Pawns are steadfast companions of the Arisen, helping him in combat and sometimes in other matters. **They assume the role of nPCs traveling with the hero, with the party members forming something like a close-knit team.** Pawns are independent to a degree, but they can also be controlled and directed via commands issued by the player.

In DD2, the Pawn mechanic has been expanded compared to the first installment of the series. **In the new entry, party members may point the player's attention to points of interest on the map or remind of events.** During battles, they will also provide tips, for example, show weak areas of specific enemies. **Pawns may learn skills and specializations, e.g. the ability to translate elvish.**

how to get Pawns?

Your first Pawn will be your most important companion when playing *Dragons Dogma 2*. **You will create this character in the character creation screen and he will accompany you from that point on.**

To learn more about what vocations the Pawn can assume, read All vocations (classes) page of our guide.

Aside from the main Pawn, **during combat sequences, you can summon 2 additional Pawns that are chosen from the pool of player-created Pawns.** The network functions of DD2 allow players to exchange Pawns. **You will do this from the so-called Riftstones**, which are found in most human settlements. Interacting with the stone will give you access to a special space where you will be able to hire, return, and also check the available Pawns in the game.

If during the game, you'll cross paths with Pawns whose help was indispensable and who complemented your team well, you'll be able to add these companions to your list of favourite Pawns.

best vocation for Pawn

A good idea when creating a Pawn will be to make him of a vocation that supports your character class and playstyle. If, for example, you are playing as an Archer, consider creating a Pawn-Fighter that will stand on the frontline while you take out targets from a distance. If your class excels at melee combat, your ally can take the form of a Mage that will help you stay alive, casting healing spells or debuffs on your enemies.

The key to success here is creating a balanced team so you can respond to various dangers, so when choosing Pawns made by other players, pay attention to whether you can match them to play in your team. Creating a well-versed nPC team specializing in different aspects of combat will help you prevail even when faced with multi-faceted threat.

best specialization for Pawn

In DD2, Pawns can have specific specializations. here are all of them:

1. **Logistician** - Pawn willingly combines materials owned by the party and skillfully manages the equipment by transferring it between party members;
2. **hawker** - operates on principles similar to a wandering merchant and allows you to sell certain items to them;
3. **Forager** - marks and finds useful items on the map to improve your equipment;
4. **Chirurgeon** - Pawn eagerly uses healing items and ensures the good condition of the Arisen and the rest of the party;
5. **Woodland Wordsmith** - Pawn understands and translates elvish speech for the Arisen;
6. **Aphonite** - Pawn is not very eager to speak and is mostly silent.

All specializations available in the game (except for the rather useless Aphonite) offer tangible benefits and will certainly come in handy during your journeys. **The most important thing is to choose a Pawn with the appropriate specialization for the specific mission**. If, for example, you assume that during your next trip you may meet elves, then a translator with the Woodland Wordsmith skill will prove to be invaluable help.

bestiary, all bosses

The world of DD2 is inhabited by diverse and dangerous creatures. On this page we will present you with an overview of each of them, as well as give you tips on how to fight them.

1. Common animals **patrolling forests and mountains** that hunt in groups.
2. Wolves are the most common predatory animals in the game, hunting in packs. **They spend most of the battles away from you - they attack once and run away**. however, they can pin down you or your Pawns and bite repeatedly.

3. **To deal with the wolves, eliminate them one by one.** Once you hit the wolf with an attack, it will be hard for it to escape from your blade, so continue until the enemy is dead.

Skeletons

1. Remnants of warriors marked by a curse. **They move extremely fast.**
2. **You will encounter skeletons at night - they can emerge from the ground unexpectedly.** There is not much to say about them, they are fairly simple opponents armed with conventional weapons. **After defeating them, remember to destroy their remains with an additional blow so that they do not rise again.**

Specters

1. **Aggressive spirits that can possess people.**
2. **Specters appear at night and their main attack is to posses characters - they do not deal much damage, but they do drain your stamina.** For this reason, they do not pose a significant threat on their own, but they can be dangerous in combination with other enemies, as an exhausted hero cannot effectively defend themselves.
3. Specters are very agile and hard to hit. **Single, powerful attacks such as Weapon Arts are most effective against them.**

Saurians

1. Lizard-like people living in colonies near water. They use long spears. **When fighting them, it is worth attacking their tails.**

2. **Saurians are quite dangerous opponents, usually attacking in groups of two or three.** They are very resistant to damage and have a large attack range thanks to their spears.

3. **To deal with the Saurians, attack them from behind.** A few attacks will cut off their tail, which will stun them and significantly lower their defense - you can then easily finish them off.

Chopper

1. A type of goblin hiding deep in the forests. **They specialize in organizing ambushes**, during which they use their numbers and agility.

2. **The only major difference between Choppers and Goblins is that they attack unexpectedly, camouflaging themselves among their surroundings.** Once you locate them, they shouldn't cause you any problems.

Cyclops

A massive beast of great strength. Their aggressive nature often becomes a cause for fighting.

1. **Cyclops is the first real boss you will encounter in *Dragons Dogma 2*.** You will encounter him together with Gregor on the way to the capital. Since this is the

first large enemy you will encounter, it is also the weakest of them - **it only has two health bars and is easy to take down.**

2. **A good way to deal with this type of opponent is to attack his weak point - their single eye.** You can do this by using ranged attacks or by climbing onto the monster. **Stick to the enemy's back - he attacks mainly by swinging his club in front of himself.** It's best to climb the cyclops from behind - **be careful when you're climbing on his lower half, because the enemy can sit down and crush you.** Once you climb onto the cyclops's back, you should be safe. **Once you've knocked down the cyclops, you can get up to his face and attack - stick your weapon in its eye, dealing massive damage.**

Ogre

1. A humanoid, hairy creature **that is exceptionally fast for its size.** It is said that he has a taste for kidnapping and devouring women.

2. **Ogres are quite common, but also dangerous bosses.** In battle, they use their paws and make jumps - for example, they can jump onto a wall and then try to crush you with their weight. **They have three health bars.**

3. **The ogre's weakness is quite non-obvious, and it is women. If you have a female character in your party, the ogre will prioritize her in combat, trying to grab her.** If he manages to do this, he will start covering the character with corrosive saliva - he is then almost completely defenseless and the rest of the party can attack him.

4. **It's best to climb ogres from the front** - stay behind the monster during the fight and try to get between its legs to climb on top of it. **If you climb up from behind, there is a high chance that the ogre will jump and try to crush you against the ground or wall.**

Minotaur

1. **Bull-headed beasts**. They wield huge axes, and their charge can easily knock down even the strongest warrior.

2. **Minotaurs deal a lot of damage, but are easily staggered and knocked down**. In the fight against this beast, beware of the sweeping axe swings, which can reach even behind the Minotaur's back. The enemy can also charge at you with horns. **Minotaurs are vulnerable to ice, and their powerful horns are also their weakness - a good blow to the head or a throw of a stone will stagger the beast and may even break off its horn**. Minotaurs have as many as four health bars, but they quickly fall to the ground if you keep attacking them.

3. **Climb the Minotaurs from behind and make sure you have plenty of stamina. The monster will try to throw you off by getting down on all fours and kicking wildly.** If you manage to grab to him, you can climb on his head and attack.

Griffin

1. **Giant hybrids of Lion and eagle**. They circle the sky to suddenly attack their prey from above.

2. **Unlike other bosses, fights with Griffins are often unexpected because they like to attack by surprise**. They can descend from the sky when you are busy fighting opponents or even another boss. They have five health bars and **after a while they escape, flying back to their nest**.

3. **During a fight, a Griffin can grab a party member and throw them from a great height**.

Chimera

A grotesque abomination with three heads - a lion, a goat and a snake. Each of them has a different attack pattern, and together they have the ability to bite, use spells, and poison.

Drake

A cousin of dragons. **In addition to the ability to breathe fire, it also uses magic.** When encountering this enemy on your path, you should prepare for a tough fight.

Dullahan

The undead knight shrouded in a mysterious flame, holding his own head in his hands. **A master swordsman with great melee skills.**

Golem

An artificial form of life created with magic. The hard shell made of rock absorbs magical and physical attacks. **however, their bodies are decorated with glowing points, which are a Golem's weak point**.

hobgoblins

A stronger and smarter variant of Goblins. Their larger size and mastery in using weapons make them dangerous opponents.

Knacker

Another tribe of Goblins. bigger and specializing in the use of long weapons. **They like to attack using a terrain difference**.

Rattlers

Giant toads covered with stones. They inhabit warm, mountainous canyons. **When fighting them, try to flip them on their backs to expose their sensitive underbelly**.

Slimes

Gooey creatures capable of dissolving organic matter. **Physical attacks won't hurt them, so it's a good idea to use magic against them.**

Talos

A brown giant spreading devastation after coming out of the sea. To fight him effectively, **you will need to climb the metal parts of his body.**

Undead

Corpses forced to move by evil forces. **They are vulnerable to fire and holy attacks.**

Wight

A soul of a priest that came into live. **Difficult to fight due to their ability to fly and a wide variety of dangerous spells.**

All Portcrystals locations

Portcrystals are special places in Dragons Dogma 2 that act as fast travel hubs in the game. On this page we will show you the location of each of them.

The fast travel system in *Dragons Dogma 2* is very limited. **nevertheless, In addition to the slow and dangerous ox carts that traverse the roads between settlements, you can use Portcrystals - special stations that serve as safe, instant teleportation destinations.** On this page of our guide, we provide the location of every Portcrystal to find in the world, as well as show how to get the portable ones.

- Portcrystal in Vernworth (fixed)
- Portcrystal in harve village (fixed)
- Portcrystal for completing Feast of Deception
- Portcrystal for solving Sphinx's puzzles
- Portcrystal for completing Trial of Archery
- Portcrystal in the Griffin's nest
- Portcrystal bought from The Dragonforged

Portcrystal in Vernworth (fixed)

The first of the Portcrystals in the game can be found in the central part of Vernworth - the northern human kingdom's capital. Its exact location is south-west from a large building with a Riftstone, right next to the inn and guild headquarters. **Try to activate it during the first visit to the city** to have the option to teleport to the capital ready at all times.

You can read more about various means of fast travel on a dedicated page of our guide.

Portcrystal in harve village (fixed)

The second and also the last stationary Portcrystal is located on a small peninsula in the town of harve village, due west from the capital. Look for it in the southern part of the city, near the sea shore.

Portcrystal for completing Feast of Deception

The first of portable Portcrystals is received in the course of the main story. After completing all tasks received from Captain brant in vernworth, one of the final missions in the capital will reward you with a portable, multi-use Portcrystal.

Portcrystal for solving Sphinx's puzzles

The first location where you encounter the Sphinx is northeast of the border crossing between vermund and battahl. For completing his **Riddle of Madness**, you'll be rewarded with another portable Portcrystal.

1. **When asked about your "Most beloved", present your main Pawn**. Grab him and place on the platform before the Sphinx.

Interestingly enough, when solving the next of Sphinx's riddles, with a little slyness, you can receive a second Portcrystal. **Any item chosen from your inventory in Riddle of Conviction will be duplicated**. Select the Portcrystal you've just received in the previous riddle to get another one. There aren't any bad answers in this riddle, but remember to choose a valuable item for duplication.

Portcrystal for completing Trial of Archery

After reaching the end of Vernworth plotline (completing Seat of the Sovra quest) and completing Gift of the bow task, **you'll be able to start another quest featuring Glyndwren**. The task will lead you to Sacred Arbor village - a hidden elven village. **You will have to fight an Ogre to save Glyndwren's sister. Your reward for this will be another Portcrystal.**

In the elven village, a Pawn with Woodland Wordsmith specialization will be useful, as he can translate the incomprehensive elvish language.

Portcrystal in the Griffin's nest

Another Portcrystal can be found in Griffin's nest. The beast's dwelling is in the mist-covered Misty Marches region which is found in western Vermund. To get the treasure he hoards, you'll need to defeat him, so be ready for a tough encounter in a hostile area.

Portcrystal bought from The Dragonforged

The last Portcrystal can be purchased from an nPC known as The Dragonforged. he resides in bay Wayside Shrine in the country of battahl. To buy his stock, among it many rare items, you need Wrymslife Crystals. **These, in turn, will be obtained during the later missions of the main story when fighting dragons.**

FAQ

Important Choices

Go to the capital with Gregor or alone?

Will you accompany me to the capital? One of the first main quests in DD2 requires you to travel to Vernworth, the capital of the state of Vermund. On this page we have described one of the first choices in the game - whether to head to the capital alone or together with Gregor.

Dragon's Wake is the title of one of the first story quests in *Dragons Dogma 2*. During it, you'll visit Melve, a small village, experience a flashback where Arisen is facing the dragon, and finally embark to Vernworth, the capital of Vermund. **During the latter part of the quest, you'll need to make a choice - either continue the journey to the capital alone or join Gregor by boarding a cart. On this page of our guide, we describe both choices and explain what each choice entails.**

- When the choice appears?
- Should I go to the capital with Gregor?
- Should I go to the capital alone?

When the choice appears?

1. **You will make the decision in question after a scripted battle against a cyclops and having opened the way forward.** Your actions have impressed Gregor, who will no longer see the need of keeping an eye on you. now, you can continue the journey to the capital alone, or join Gregor by boarding a cart. **no matter what decision you make, you will eventually reach the capital** - but the journey sequence itself will be different.

Should I go to the capital with Gregor?

1. **If you decide to continue the journey with Gregor, you must sit next to him in the cart.** Your character will go to sleep and wake up already before the gates of vernworth. There is a possibility that you will encounter a goblin ambush along the way, but with the help of Gregor and his men, you should be able to handle them easily. **This option is simpler, faster and recommended for beginner players.**

Should I go to the capital alone?

1. **If you decide to travel to the capital alone, you will travel on foot, accompanied by your pawns. This option is definitely more challenging.** The journey is long, and there are no settlements on the way to vernworth - so there are also no inns. While you'll come across a few bonfires, there's no guarantee you'll find camp kits - if you don't have a few on hand, **your maximum health may**

take a serious hit cause of the large number of enemies you'll encounter along the way.

2. About halfway there, you'll come across an optional cave that you can explore. There are many Saurians, bandits, and also a powerful ogre hiding there. There is a lot of gold in the cave, but you must be ready for challenging battles. **Just before reaching Vernworth, we also came across another ogre on the side of the main road. He was accompanied in battle by goblins and harpies who could put heroes to sleep.** Gregor's absence means that you can only count on yourselves and your pawns.

1. **Since the journey is long, there is a high probability that night will come with you still along the way.** Traveling at night means having to use lanterns and additional dangerous enemies appearing, such as skeletons and specters.
2. **Traveling to the capital alone is challenging, but you'll be rewarded for it with additional gold and experience.** With the accumulated wealth and skill points, you can learn new skills in guild headquarters or buy better equipment from the smith and armorer in Vernworth. **As a result, choosing to continue alone in *Dragons Dogma 2* is an option for advanced or confident in their skill players.**

Should I give gold to Sven?

Sven is a mysterious young man whom you will meet shortly after you start playing DD2. On this page we will give you a hint whether it is worth interacting with him.

After arriving in Vernworth, the capital of the human kingdom, you will meet Sven - **a mysterious boy running away from a guard.** He asks you for help, and over the next few days you will have several opportunities to meet him in various situations. **On this page, we will explain the origin of this character and whether it is worth helping him.**

- First meeting with Sven
- Should I give Sven some money?
- What does helping Sven do?

First meeting with Sven

After arriving in Vernworth and having the first conversation with Brant, go out onto the street. You will watch a short cut-scene showing a boy running away from a guard. **You can point out the guard to the hiding boy or confuse him to help the boy.** If you choose the second option, **Sven will thank you for your help and promise that you will meet again someday.**

Should I give Sven some money?

The second meeting with Sven will happen sometime later. **You'll find him arguing at one of the stalls near the city gates.** The young man will recognize you and **ask you to lend him 1,000 gold to buy a trinket**. If you agree to lend him money, the boy will make a purchase and promise that he will soon repay his debt. **This event will activate a quest, during which you will meet with Sven every few days and he will pay off part of the debt.**

What does helping Sven do?

The following section contains minor plot spoilers.

During the meetings, the boy will share various interesting facts about himself with you. **You will learn, among other things, that Sven is actually a resident of the royal palace, and he sneaks out onto the streets to avoid the tutelage of his strict mother - Queen Vermund.**

however, Sven's usefulness does not end with providing you information about the world. **During one of the missions involving infiltrating the royal castle, the boy can come to your aid and distract the guards, which will make the task much easier.**

During one of the last meetings, Sven will once again thank you for your kindness and **will give you 4,000 gold pieces and a set of richly decorated clothes.** Therefore, it can be safely assumed that the small price associated with helping Sven pays off in the later stages of the game.

Let the spy go or not?

Your activities in DD2 have brought a spy on your tail. In the quest The Arisen's Shadow you will be faced with a choice - capture the spy or let him go for a fee. On the guide page we described the consequences of the decision.

After arriving in Vernworth, the main story of *Dragons Dogma 2* revolves around missions received from Captain Brant. **After completing several such tasks, one of your pawns will warn you that you are being followed by someone.** This will start The Arisen's Shadow quest. **On this page of our guide, we show how to catch the spy and what to do when you catch him.**

- how to catch the spy?

- What to do with the spy?

how to catch the spy?

1. **The spy will start following you after completing some of Captain brant's missions.** Your pawns will let you know about his presence. **he won't be marked on your map, so you need to spot him on your own.** The spy, bermudo, wear a brown hood and will attempt to hide from your gaze. **Look for a character that starts to run away when you look at him - this is the spy.**

2. **To capture bermudo, you need to go after him - fortunately, inside the city, your stamina is infinite, which means infinite sprint.** If you are too encumbered to run, temporarily transfer your equipment to your pawns. **Once you get close to the spy, grab him and hold the sprint button to pin him to the ground.**

What to do with the spy?

1. The spy will try to explain himself and ask to be allowed to leave. **You can refuse or demand money in exchange for releasing him.**

2. **If you refuse, bermudo will attack you. Fight him - after a moment, Captain brant should intervene, who will arrest the spy.** The captain asks you to return in a few days after he is done interrogating bermudo. **Proceed with other affairs and return after the said time. brant will reveal that bermudo is a battahl spy and reward you with 4,000G. This event will end the quest.**

Warning - if you kill the spy before brant makes it, the quest will stall. To finish it, you will have to use the Wakestone and resurrect bermudo. If the spy's health falls to a dangerous level, try to pin him to the ground again and hold until the captain appears.

1. **If you demand money, bermudo will offer you 5,000 G** - you can accept the money or refuse and ask for more. The latter option will make bermudo attack. **If you accept the money, the spy will pay you and leave. This will end the quest - you can go to Captain brant and tell him about the incident.** After a few days, he will learn the identity of the spy and share the information, but you won't receive any gold as a reward.

2. **In the end, taking money from the spy will yield better rewards** - provided you feel comfortable with letting a mysterious agent who spied on you free.

Should I reveal the beggar's secret?

In the capital of vermund you will come across the task A baggers Tale in Dragons Dogma 2. You are faced with a choice - what to do with the evidences. On this page of the guide we describe the consequences of each possible decision.

A beggar's Tale is the name of one of the quests in *Dragon Dogma 2* that can be initiated in vernworth - the human capital city. **During the task, you'll shadow a mysterious beggar and learn his most kept secret.** On this page of our guide, we show how to learn the secret as well as explain the consequences following 3 different endings to the mission

- how to follow beggar Albert?
- Giving the evidence to Albert
- Giving the evidence to hilda
- Giving the evidence to Celina

how to follow beggar Albert?

The beggars Tale quest is activated automatically after benton, a beggar found in the city's main square, talks to you. he will tell you about the strange behavior of Albert, another beggar, who spends his daytime telling stories by the fountain. **benton will ask you to investigate the matter, initiating the said task.**

Albert has a unique day/night activity that learning will help you uncover the secret. **At the end of the day, when the sun is about to set, Albert will leave his post at the fountain and start heading towards the slums.** Follow him until he stops at an inn.

Albert doesn't suspect that he is being followed, so you don't have to sneak or hide excessively. Just make sure you stay a few meters behind him and don't get in his way.

The target will spend the evening in the inn. During that time, he will meet with his wife Cecilia. **After a few drinks, he will head to his house in the eastern part of the city. Follow him.** When he enters the apartment, wait a few moments. he will leave the house. Interestingly, this time he will be dressed in expensive, richly decorated robes.

enter his house and steal beggars Garb - proof of Albert's secret. With the item in your inventory, you can decide how to end the quest.

Giving the evidence to Albert

The next morning, you can return to Albert's house. You will find the flustered man at the door. If you give him the evidence, he will ask you to keep the secret to yourself. **In return, you will receive 5,000 gold pieces, and the quest will be marked as complete.**

Giving the evidence to hilda

An alternative option to solve the mission is to give the evidence to hilda - Albert's lover. The woman resides in a building in the eastern part of the rich district. After giving her beggars Garb, the woman will be outraged by Albert's double life and will vow to confront him with this news. If you return to hilda a day later, the satisfied woman will reveal to you that the embarrassed Albert stopped pretending to be a beggar and returned to his old job. **In exchange for your help, you will receive some experience and 3 pieces of Onyx.**

Giving the evidence to Celina

The last and the most heartbreaking way to solve the mission is to give the evidence to Celina - Albert's wife from the slums. You will find the woman in the tavern where Albert was the night before. The woman, confronted with the lie, will be very saddened. If you visit the house of the false beggar a day later, you'll find guards there who will inform you that the heartbroken Celina killed her husband and then took her life. **Your reward will be 3000 gold and noonbloom flower.**

Vocations

How to change vocation?

Vocations are the equivalent of character classes in the DD2 world. On this page, we'll walk you through the process that will allow you to switch between them and test new styles of gameplay.

In *Dragons Dogma 2*, you will have access to 10 different vocations offering a variety of gameplay styles and approaches to fighting as a party. Capcom's latest game takes a very liberal approach to changing the active character class, giving players the opportunity to experiment without fear of consequences. **On this page, we will tell you how to change your vocation and what this process involves.**

- how to unlock all vocations?
- how to change a vocation in the Guild?

How to unlock all vocations?

When creating a character in DD2, you will be asked to choose one out of four vocations. These are:

1. **Archer (bow);**
2. **Fighter (sword and shield);**
3. **Mage (magic);**
4. **Thief (daggers).**

Although they are called "basic" in the game, these classes are in no way inferior to more complicated vocations and can be used until the end of the game.

Quite early in the game, you will be **able to unlock 2 advanced vocations**. These are:

1. **Warrior (heavy two-handed weapon);**
2. **Sorcerer (offensive magic).**

You can find the process of unlocking the mentioned vocations on a separate page of our guide: how to unlock Warrior and Sorcerer vocations.

In the later stages of the game, you will gradually unlock new vocations called hybrid vocations. Among them you will find:

1. Mystic Spearhand **(a combination of spear combat and magic);**
2. Magick Archer **(combination of bow fighting and magic);**
3. Trickster **(using the censer to control and confuse enemies);**
4. Warfarer (combination of several features of the other classes).

hybrid vocations combine elements characteristic of other, more basic classes. In this way, they offer an interesting modification within a similar gameplay style. For advice related to unlocking each hybrid vocation, check out separate guide pages in the links above.

how to change a vocation in the Guild?

Changing the vocation is possible in the Guild building. Appropriate facilities are located in most of the larger cities and are marked with a coat of arms with two swords.

Approach the employee standing behind the counter. **From the available options, select "Change vocation" and choose the class that interests you**. Changing vocation is associated with a fairly symbolic fee of 150 or 200 DCP.

You use DCP points when developing class and basic skills. DCP are received by defeating enemies, completing tasks, and leveling up vocations.

After changing the vocation, you will also be equipped with basic equipment for a specific class. You can use it to test new skills, but if you plan to stay with the new class for longer, we suggest buying better equipment from one of the traders. The situation is similar with testing new class skills. **Before you spend your entire pool of DCPs on improving the skills for a new vocation, check whether you like the new play style**. A few test fights should give you an insight into what playing as the new class looks like.

How to unlock Mystic Spearhand?

Mystic Spearhand is one of the classes in DD2, being a hybrid between a warrior and a mage. However, it is not available from the beginning of the game. On this page we described how to unlock the Mystic Spearhand class.

Mystic Spearhand is one of the new classes added to *Dragons Dogma 2*. This is a hybrid class wielding a spear, relying on both melee combat and magic. **The class is special and can only be used by the playable hero** - Pawn can't use it. However, it is not available from the beginning of the game, and unlocking it requires some work. On this page of the guide, we described how to unlock the Mystic Spearhand class.

how to unlock Mystic Spearhand?

1. **To unlock the Mystic Spearhand class, you must reach Vernworth, the capital of Vermund, and continue the main storyline.** You will have to perform several tasks for Brant, the captain of the guard. **Once you have dealt with a few of his tasks, you must return to Melve. The easiest way is to go by Oxcart** - the perfect excuse is, for example, the Oxcart Courier side mission, during which you have to return to Melve using Oxcart to deliver a letter.
2. **When you return, you will see that the ruins of Melve have been attacked by a dragon again. You must help the village's defenders repel the attack** - fortunately, the beast will escape after depleting a few of its health bars.
3. After the battle, look around among the crowd. **There will be a hooded individual with a spear on his back - that's Sigurd. Talk to him, and he will teach you his fighting style. This will unlock Mystic Spearhand** - you can now purchase this class at any guild headquarters in exchange for a small amount of discipline points.

how to unlock Warrior and Sorcerer vocations?

Warrior and Sorcerer are advanced vocations in DD2. On this page of the guide we will tell you when and where you can unlock them. Warrior and Sorcerer are classes that are an evolution of basic vocations and the game describes them as "Advanced vocations". **Unlocking these vocations is somewhat of a "major step" in what can be treated as a natural development path for some heroes.** On this page of our guide, we provide all needed information and describe the requirements that need to be met to unlock the aforementioned character classes.

how to complete the "Vocation Frustration" quest?

To receive the quest about unlocking the new vocations, **you'll need to visit the Guild headquarters in the capital of Vermund**. The building is right next to the Inn, near the city marketplace. **Talk to the man behind the counter, Klaus, who will share a story involving stolen transport containing Archstaff and Greatsword.** As can be expected, your task will be to retrieve these weapons, and completing this task will unlock the new vocations.

Klaus will send you to the smith Roderic. You can recognize his stall thanks to a sword emblem. Look for it on the square with the statue. **The blacksmith will show you the way to the goblins' hideout.** It is located west of Vernworth. The road to the objective is quite long, so before embarking, we recommend replenishing supplies and resting.

Leave the city through the west gate and follow the mission marker. Keep to the beaten path. however, be on your guard, because on the way you will encounter many hostile creatures such as harpies or goblins. It's possible that you'll also encounter a cyclops.

After reaching the camp, look for the entrance to the caves. In the dark corridors, you will encounter large groups of aggressive goblins. **Some of them may attempt surprise attacks, so thread lightly.** The cave system is quite extensive, but the layout is not complicated. **Follow the main corridor forward until you reach a larger room full of enemies, bonfires, and treasure chests.** examine the contents of every chest carefully, as two of them hide the sought weapons. Take them and return to the city.

The chest with Greatsword is in a room protected by a locked door. The Archstaff, on the other hand, is hidden below the bridge in the large northern room.

After retrieving the items and delivering them to Klaus in Guild headquarters, **both Advanced vocations will become available**.

Quest

Do quests have a time limit?

DD2 places great emphasis on immersion. The game world is alive and changes independently of the player's actions. On this page we have described whether the quests in the game are time-limited and whether exceeding the limit results in consequences.

Dragons Dogma 2 is set in a huge, immersive world where action and consequence play a major role and the player is just one of many inhabitants. The world evolves and changes even without your input, and same applies to quests. **On this page of our guide, we explain whether the quests in the game have an imposed time limit and whether the player may suffer consequences for delaying completion of them.**

- Do quests have a time limit?
- What are the consequences of exceeding the time limit?

Do quests have a time limit?

Yes - in *Dragons Dogma 2*, most quests have a limited window to complete them. Many of the quests will require almost immediate action to complete them successfully. This is made in order to achieve immersion and make the player understand that he is only one of the parties inhabiting this living, changing world. **Most of the time-limited quests won't mention or show a counter of the remaining time to complete, so you need to be vigilant and try to avoid putting quests for later, especially if the task seems urgent.**

What are the consequences of exceeding the time limit?

The consequences of not completing the quest on time differ, but are always negative. One of the exemplary time-limited quests is saving a child lost in the forest. If the player does not find the child within a few days, he will end being killed by wild animals. **Depending on the task, failure may result in being unable to claim the reward or the ensuing death of a potentially important nPC.** Therefore, optimal quest management is crucial - **don't accept too many tasks at once, as you risk running out of time to complete them.**

Where to find Fruit Roborant for the little girl in Melve?

In the beginning stage of DD2, in the village of Melve, you will meet a girl asking you for Fruit Roborant. On this page of the guide we have described how to get this medicine and what rewards you will receive for handing it over.

During your stay in Melve, one of the first settlements you'll encounter, you may be approached by Flora, a girl who asks for help in providing her with a Fruit

Roborant, a type of medicinal item. **On this page of our guide, we show where to obtain the medicine and what rewards you'll get for delivering it.**

- What is Fruit Roborant and how to obtain it?
- Should I give Flora Fruit Roborant?

What is Fruit Roborant and how to obtain it?

1. **Fruit Roborant is a medicine that restores lost health points.** It is more expensive, but also better than the basic healing potion in the game, which is Salubrious Draught. **There are two main ways to obtain Fruit Roborant - purchasing it from a merchant or crafting. In Melve, Fruit Roborant is sold by the pharmacist who lives in the building next to Flora.** he will sell you this remedy for 600 G per piece.

2. **Another way to obtain Fruit Roborant is crafting. You can craft it at any time if you have two needed ingredients - Dried Fruit and any green herb.** herbs are easily found when exploring the world, but getting Dried Fruit requires a bit more work. Dried Fruit are crafted from any two Ripened fruit - for food to get this status, it has to remain in your inventory for a few days. **To craft it, simply mix two Ripened fruit in the crafting menu (e.g. x1 Ripened Apple, x1 Ripened Grape or 2x Ripened Apple) - this will create Dried Fruit,** which on its own has the same effect as a healing potion. **Continue by mixing Dried Fruit with any green herb to get Fruit Roborant.**

Should I give Flora Fruit Roborant?

1. **Although Fruit Roborant is a valuable healing item, we recommend giving it to Flora. Delivering it will be rewarded with 100 G and Ring of exultation**, a ring that increases your max health by 100. **This ring normally costs 1,000 G, so if you buy Fruit Roborant and give it to a girl, you will still save 500 G thanks to the exchange**.
2. however, the ring is not the only reward. **Some time later, when you arrive at the capital of the kingdom - the city of vernworth - you will meet Auriol, Flora's grandfather, in the market. he will be grateful for your help and will offer you a permanent 20% discount in his store**. Auriol is an apothecary who sells useful healing items, such as Fruit Roborant - **helping Flora will definitely pay off**.

Where is the room with books?

The task of finding a room full of books is one of the requirements thrown to the player in the main plot of DD2. On this page we will explain to you how to find this place and how to release Judge Waldhar.

While completing The Caged Magistrate, one of your objectives is to find a room full of books that will meet the strict requirements of the imprisoned judge. even if the provided description alone seems a bit enigmatic, thanks to our help, you'll quickly find the place in question. **below we list actions that need to be completed for the quest to end successfully.**

- Where to find Judge Waldhar?
- how to complete The Caged Magistrate quest?
- how to get Judge Waldhar out of the dungeon?

Where to find Judge Waldhar?

After receiving the briefing from Captain Brant, proceed to Verworth's southern district. After passing through the northern gate, head to the eastern part of the palace complex. **There will be a tower located behind the ox stable.** Enter it and follow the stairs down.

The palace complex is a restricted area, your Pawns will not be able to enter it. Companions will return to you when you leave the area.

The guards patrolling the dungeons will attack you if they spot you. Fortunately, their sight range is poor, so all you need to do is stay a few meters away. However, try not to run into them. **Judge Waldhar is in the first cell on the right. Open it with the key received from the captain.** In the conversation with the judge, he will ask you to prepare a room full of books for him. After receiving the new mission objective, leave the dungeon.

During the infiltration of the palace and other places where entry is forbidden, you can make your task easier by wearing a Marcher set - Marcher's helm, Marcher's Armor and Marcher's Cuisses. This is the armor worn by castle guards, so you will look like one of them, which should prevent the guards from attacking you if they detect you. In the vicinity of the castle and in some castle rooms, there are several chests, each of which hides a separate set of this armor.

how to complete The Caged Magistrate quest?

Return to the Captain in the tavern and report your progress. **Brant will send you to the slums located in the western part of the city.** In the small square, you will encounter Kendrick - an older man dressed in blue robes. Give him a donation and he will ask you for a favour. **Your task will be to find a missing boy - Malcolm.**

To learn more about Malcolm's whereabouts, you need to find a girl named Aimee first. If it is currently nighttime, you should find her sleeping in a large building in the center of the slums. Aimee will reveal that Malcolm embarked on a quest to explore the crypts located underneath the city. **With the new findings, report back to Kendrick.**

Kendrick will ask you for help in exploring the crypt. Follow him to the crypt entrance next to tower ruins. The crypts layout is not complicated, so you should come across the missing boy quite quickly. **A cut-scene will be initiated where Malcolm leads you to a found room filled to the brim with books and scrolls.** This place should be perfect for Waldhar. **Report back to Captain brant and the next stage of the quest will be to rescue the judge from his dungeon cell.**

how to get Judge Waldhar out of the dungeon?

Go back to the dungeon where Judge Waldhar is staying. Share with him the information about the room. The man will ask you for help to get out of the dungeon.

The corridor is guarded by two sentries that patrol the room by walking around it in a circular fashion. **They are not very observant, so all you need to do is wait for them to pass the cell, and then slowly start moving right. Avoid being detected by the guards by hiding behind pillars and make sure that the judge is following you.**

After emerging from the corridor, you'll encounter bars that can be opened with the key obtained from the Captain. Go down the stairs until you reach another grate that leads to the seashore. Use the key again, and you'll open the way out.

Judge Waldhar will thank you for your help and leave. The task is now complete - you can return and brief Captain brants.

how to steal the queen's letter?

Stealing the letter with evidence of the queen's manipulation is the goal of Disas Plot quest in DD2. This page will give you tips on how to avoid detection in the castle and how to get out of the castle.

One of the missions received from Captain brant in vermouth involves sneaking into the palace grounds and stealing a letter which will be evidence of the nefarious scheming of the false queen. The task is of a sneaking sort, and some directions provided by the game may be a bit enigmatic. On this page of our guide, we provide a few tips that will make completing Disa's Plot quest easier.

how to complete Disa's Plot quest?

The first step will be to initiate the task by talking to Captain brant in the inn. After asking about the queen-regent, the man will reveal his suspicions to you and order you to steal a letter that will incriminate the false ruler. The mission marker will lead you to the vernworth palace grounds in the southern part of the city.

As you enter the palace territory, you'll be greeted by Sonia, a guard and a trusted associate of brant. Sonia will take you to a side entrance intended for royal guards which will allow you to enter the building undetected.

Inside the next room you'll find a chest that contains a full set of palace guard armor. equip it to blend into the crowd and avoid being exposed. **The outfit doesn't have any class restrictions and can be equipped by any character.** If you feel for it, you can use the opportunity to do some exploring around the palace and loot some treasure.

For the purpose of the quest, proceed to the main throne room. Locate a spiral staircase located near one of the walls of the room and use them to climb one floor up. Go to the western part of the floor. The mission marker will help you locate the sought room.

Inside, you'll find what you came for - a fragment of the queen's letter lying on the desk. **Unexpectedly, your snooping around will be interrupted by the appearance of the queen's son - Sven.** If you helped him earlier and lent him money, he will gladly help you by distracting the guards. You can learn more about the lending and Sven on a dedicated page of our guide.

After the boy distracts the guards, quickly vault through the open window to find yourself in the castle courtyard. Quickly leave the palace grounds and report to brant waiting in the inn. **brant will reward you with a lot of gold and a Wakestone.**

how to buy a house?

Owning your own house in DD2 is a very big gameplay convenience. On this page, we'll tell you how to complete the quest A Place to Call home, and in the process, how to take possession of a house.

One of the advantages of owning a private house in DD2 is the ability to spend the night without having to pay a fee. Although obtaining the deed is a costly endeavour, the investment will quickly return itself. **On this page of our guide, we show how to unlock the quest that will give you the opportunity to own a property.**

- buying a house in Vernworth
- buying a house in bakbattahl
- What are the advantages of having a private house in Dragons Dogma 2?

buying a house in Vernworth

For the option to buy a house in the human capital city to be available, you need to initiate and complete the A Place to Call home quest. To start the mission, approach Mildred, a woman who can often be found on a street west from the main marketplace. You don't have to interact with her - she will talk to you on her own and during the conversation explain that she is soon to take a trip and searches for a person who will take care of her house in the meantime.

Mildred should appear in this location already in earlier stages of the game. If the woman doesn't talk to you on her own, try to complete some quests for Captain brant. his quests often initiate various events such as the appearance of important nPCs in the city.

Mildred will lead you to a house located nearby, thank you, and leave the city. For the next 7 days, you can use the home as it was your property. You can sleep in it, and also use the private chest located inside.

The woman will return to the city after 7 days. **She will announce that she is planning to move and leave you with an offer - to buy her Vernworth house for**

20,000 gold. Although the price may seem steep if you received this offer in the initial stage of the game, the investment should pay off for you after about just 10 nights. **Remember - spending one night in the vernworth inn costs 2,000g.**

If you accept Mildred's offer, the woman will give you ownership of the building and leave the city. From now on, the house is yours, and you can use the facilities as you see fit.

If you are interested in the offer, but currently don't have the necessary money, you can raise the needed gold (there isn't any time limit on the offer) and return to Mildred at a later time. The woman's offer will remain in effect.

buying a house in bakbattahl

Purchasing property in the capital of battahl is much less complicated. **During your first visit to the city, you can go to its northern part, where you will meet a woman named Adrea.** She will approach you and bluntly ask if you would be interested in buying a house in a residential district of the capital.

Adrea will ask for 30,000 gold. If you agree, you will be immediately transferred to your new residence. From now on, you will be able to use this private space just like the one in vernworth.

What are the advantages of having a private house in Dragons Dogma 2?

house works similarly to an inn. **You can spend nights here free of charge**, and after resting, a save will be created. To learn more about the topic of saving your progress in DD2, visit a dedicated page of our guide.

The house also has a private chest where you can store your excess equipment.

how to solve the Sphinx's riddles?

The Sphinx is one of the most unique monsters in the entire game. As befits this mythological beast, confronting the Sphinx takes the form of puzzles. On this page of the guide we have described where to find the Sphinx, how to solve its puzzles and what rewards you will gain in return.

not all monster encounters in *Dragons Dogma 2* will be a test of your battle skills - one of them is a test of your creativity and memory. **The Sphinx is a unique, secret nPC, who when contested has a few unusual riddles for you. You only have one chance to solve the Sphinx's riddles** and answering them the correct way is a chance to receive valuable rewards offered by the beast. **On this page of our guide, we provide the location of the Sphinx and solutions to his riddles.**

between meetings with the Sphinx, remember to rest at inns - this way you'll be able to load your save if you haven't answered the riddle correctly, giving you a second attempt to solve the puzzle. Do not attack the Sphinx - you won't get any loot for defeating him, and you'll forfeit all puzzle rewards, as Sphinx will fly away at the end of the battle, never to come back.

- Where to find the Sphinx?
- Riddle of eyes
- Riddle of Madness
- Riddle of Wisdom
- Riddle of Conviction
- Riddle of Rumination
- Riddle of Reunion

- Riddle of Futility
- Riddle of Differentiation
- Riddle of Contest
- Riddle of Recollection
- Last challenge

Where to find the Sphinx?

1. The Sphinx's **first location is in western Vermund, in Mountain Shrine, far north from Checkpoint Rest Town - a settlement on the border between Vermund and Battahl**. We recommend embarking on the trip to find it only after the conclusion of the Vermund plotline i.e. after completing all quests from Captain Brant and being witness to the coronation of the false Sovran. **To reach the Mountain Shrine, you will have to go through the Ancient battleground location.**

2. **Once you reach the Mountain Shrine, place a Portcrystal there - one will be received from Captain Brant after completing his missions.** Placing it in the Mountain Shrine will allow you to quickly teleport to the Sphinx using Ferrystone, which will prove extremely useful during some puzzles.

3. **The Sphinx has 10 riddles to solve** - the first five can be solved in any order, the sixth begins after solving the first five ones, and the last four are given in random order.

Riddle of eyes

1. **Riddle**: bring Sphinx the most valuable item from the tunnel which it opens for you.

2. **Solution**: After initiating the riddle, Sphinx will open a tunnel for you filled with dangerous enemies. Although it is worth taking these opponents on for experience and loot, the tunnel itself and the chest at its end is a decoy. **The**

solution to the puzzle is hidden at the very beginning of the tunnel, above the entrance door - there you will find a chest containing Sealing Phial. Take it and show it to the Sphinx to solve the riddle.

3. **Reward**: Wakestone x1. **You can also keep the Sealing Phial - its power allows you to move an NPC to another place once by closing him in a vial and releasing him, which can be useful during some puzzles.**

Riddle of Madness

1. **Riddle**: bring a character with whom you have maximum Affinity to the Sphinx.

2. **Solution**: To solve this puzzle, you must bring an NPC with whom you have maximum Affinity and place him on the platform before the Sphinx. To increase Affinity with a character, you can give him gifts - if the NPC starts to blush when you talk to him, it means that you've reached the maximum Affinity with him. You can then throw this character over your shoulder (or lock them in a Sealing Phial) and teleport to the Portcrystal, which you have set up near the Sphinx. **Alternatively, you can also present your main pawn, whose Affinity with you is always at maximum, to the Sphinx.**

3. **Reward**: Portcrystal x1.

Riddle of Wisdom

1. **Puzzle**: Put in front of the Sphinx a SphinxMother, SphinxFather, or SphinxParent Pawn.

2. **Solution**: To solve this puzzle, you must bring any SphinxMother, SphinxFather or SphinxParent pawn to the Sphinx. **NOTE: This Pawn has to be created by CAPCOM - when browsing Pawns, you may encounter Pawns of the same name created by other players to make the puzzle more difficult to**

others. You can view the creator of the Pawn at the bottom of the Pawn trait list. **The Pawns you need may be recruited at Riftstone of Friendship - one of them is found near narve village.** After recruiting the appropriate pawn, place it in front of the Sphinx.

3.   **Reward**: Rift Crystals x1,200.

Riddle of Conviction

1.   **Riddle**: Give the Sphinx what you deem the most valuable.
2.   **Solution**: This puzzle is a reward in itself - show **the Sphinx any item and it will duplicate it. We recommend giving something extremely valuable** - e.g. a Portcrystal, which is very rare, or if you by some miracle, managed to get one, Unmaking Arrow that can kill any enemy in the game with a single projectile.
3.   **Reward**: The item you've given will be duplicated.

Riddle of Rumination

1.   **Riddle**: Return to the location where you've found your first Seeker Token.
2.   **Solution**: Return to the place where you've found your first Seeker's Token. Unfortunately, there isn't an easy solution to this riddle - **you need to remember where you've collected your first Seeker Token. At the location of the first Seeker Token you've obtained, there will be a Finders Token - you have seven days to get it and return to the Sphinx.** here again, the planted Portcrystal will be useful, as you can return to the Sphinx immediately after getting the Token.
3.   **Reward**: Ferrystone x3.

Riddle of Reunion

1.   **Riddle**: Find the Sphinx.

2. **Solution**: After solving the previous five puzzles, the Sphinx will fly away. You can now **retrieve the Portcrystal that you've placed in Mountain Shrine - there are no more reasons to come back here**. Time to find the new location of the Sphinx - **the monster has nested in Frontier Shrine, an area behind a mist-covered area west of Checkpoint Rest Town**. When you'll find the Sphinx, the riddle will be solved and you can proceed to the next set of puzzles. **Make sure to place a Portcrystal in Frontier Shrine**.

3. **Reward**: 100,000 G.

The next four riddles are given in random order. Before solving the final, fourth riddle, make sure that your hero is equipped with a bow - you need to change your class to Archer or Warfarer.

Riddle of Futility

1. **Riddle**: bring the valuable amphora to Maurits in bakbattahl.
2. **Solution**: The puzzle requires you to deliver a valuable amphora to a specific nPC in bakbattahl, the capital of battahl. The amphora is extremely delicate - you have to carry it all the way to the capital city and a single hit inflicted on you will break it, failing the task. **Do not risk the journey and don't deliver the amphora to Maurits - instead, deliver Maurits to the amphora. Trave to bakbattahl, find Maurits and carry him to Frontier Shrine** - either by using Sealing Phial or throw him over your shoulder and teleport to Portcrystal. Successful delivery concludes this riddle.
3. **Reward**: eternal bond - a gift that significantly increases Affinity.

Riddle of Differentiation

1. **Riddle**: Put in front of the Sphinx the correct nPC.

2. **Solution**: The Sphinx will show you an illusion of a distinct man who he wants brought to him. **There are two possible illusions and the two men shown are almost identical** - Dante has a straight scar on his eye, while Vergil has a more irregular scar on his eye. **Take a screenshot of the illusion and head to Checkpoint Rest Town, where the men are located. Bring the appropriate one to the Frontier Shrine** - use Sealing Phial or throw him over your shoulder and teleport to Portcrystal. Successful delivery concludes this riddle.

3. **Reward**: Whimsical Daydream - a weapon for the Trickster.

Riddle of Contest

1. **Riddle**: Defeat a powerful enemy while weakened.
2. **Solution:** You have to fight an opponent equipped with a ring that severely reduces your damage dealt. **To win the duel, attack the enemy until you stagger him - then pick him up and throw him into the abyss.**
3. **Reward**: Ring of Ambition - a ring that increases experience point gain.

Riddle of Recollection

1. **Riddle**: Remind Sphinx how many riddles you've successfully solved up to now.
2. **Solution**: There are several small statuettes next to the Sphinx. **Place as many statuettes in front of the monster as the number of riddles you have answered correctly so far** (of course, not counting the riddle you are answering now). Once you have set up the statues, talk to the Sphinx to confirm your answer.
3. **Reward**: Unmaking Arrow - an arrow that can instantly kill any enemy. **The game automatically saves when you fire an Unmaking Arrow - make sure that the shot doesn't miss.**

before approaching the final riddle, remember to rest at the inn (thereby saving your progress) and change your class to Archer or Warfarer.

Last challenge

1. **Riddle**: Kill the Sphinx.
2. **Solution**: After solving the last, tenth puzzle, the Sphinx will attempt to fly away and leave the game permanently, taking with it the key to the chest containing the last prize. **Use Go! command to order your pawns to attack the monster**. Do not fight the Sphinx as you would any enemy - when his health drops to a certain level, he will fly away and never come back. **Instead, after the fight begins, equip the Unmaking Arrow you obtained from the Sphinx and shoot the beast**. Don't miss. The slain Sphinx will drop the key to the last chest.
3. **Reward**: eternal Wakestone - the only such Wakestone in the game. **Despite its name, it is not permanent, and same as with other Wakestones, it is consumed after first use. however, it has a special function - it resurrects all dead nPCs in a large area around you**. This makes it the perfect remedy to Dragonsplague if you let the disease kill an entire city. **There is only one eternal Wakestone in the game, so this will only give you one chance to undo this mistake**.

What to do before the coronation?

The first point of no return in Dragons Dogma 2 is the coronation of the fake Sovran. On this page of the guide we have described what you should do before going to the coronation and what is blocked after the task is completed.

The first story arc of *Dragons Dogma 2* consists of discovering the plans of the Queen Regent Disa, and the false Sovran serving her. **After completing several** tasks assigned by your main ally, Captain Brant, he will inform you about the upcoming coronation of the usurper and suggest you pay him a visit. This is the first point of no return in the game - after passing it, the game world will change irreversibly in a certain way. **On this page of the guide, we described the point of no return, what the coronation looks like and what activities become unavailable after starting the quest.**

Point of no return

1. **Coronation becomes available after completing several quests for Captain Brant. When you bring up the topic, he will ask you to wear elegant clothes** (Courtly Tunic and Courtly breeches - you should have found these clothes by completing the previous tasks for the captain). Then, let him know when you are ready to face the impostor. **he will also warn you to take care of all your assignments before going to the coronation.**

2. **This warning suggests a point of no return - once you go to the coronation, some of the game's content will become unavailable.** The coronation will not take place until you let Brant know that you are ready, so you don't need to hurry.

1. **When attending the coronation, you won't face any difficult fights or even any decisions, only a few cut-scenes. After the coronation is over, you can explore the world again as you like.** You will also receive your first Portcrystal, which you can place anywhere to use fast travel, as well as a border pass, which will allow you to enter the neighboring country - Battahl.

2. **however, the point of no return has a major impact on quests - many of them will become unavailable.** These are all the remaining quests of Captain Brant, as well as quests in Vernworth and Melve. Ulrika's and Wilhelmina's personal

quests will also disappear from the game. It is also possible that you will lose access to tasks in harve village and in the elf village. **before you go to the coronation, you should complete all the tasks in vermund that interest you and carefully explore the entire country.** The coronation will change the setting of the game from vermund to battahl.

Romances

Are there romances?

The world of DD2 is full of more or less important nPCs, whose attitudes towards the playable hero can change. On this page we have described how to approach nPCs and whether romances are included in the game.

Similarly to the first installment of the series, *Dragon Dogma 2* utilizes the Affinity system that measures the hero's current standing with different nPCs. The higher the Affinity, the better your relations with the given nPC. however, can such relationship result in an intimate scene or a special bond? **On this page of our guide, we explain how Affinity system works and answer whether there are romances in the game.**

- how to improve Affinity with nPCs?
- Are there romances in the game?
- Can you romance your own Pawn?

how to improve Affinity with nPCs?

1. **each nPC in the game has a hidden attitude indicator towards the main character, which is called Affinity.** It symbolizes the current opinion that the

character has about you. High Affinity with certain, more important characters may result in useful benefits - for example, a friendly merchant may give you a discount on his wares, while other NPCs may gift you various items.

2. **To increase your Affinity with a given character, you need to talk to him or give him gifts.** The option to give a gift is located in the bottom right corner of the screen. It is not always available - if a certain independent character does not want to accept a gift at a given moment, come back later. **Also, remember to wait a day before giving the next gift - you don't want to waste them because only the first gift given that day will increase the character's Affinity.**

1. **Different gifts have different effects on Affinity of the given character.** In the pause menu, in history tab, you can find a journal containing all NPCs that you've met. You can check here what kinds of gifts the given character prefers.

Are there romances in the game?

1. **There are romance plotlines in the game - contrary to appearances, they are not dependent on the character's Affinity and are not very in-depth.** So don't count on game-long romances in the style of *Baldur's Gate 3* or *The Witcher 3*. **Romances in *Dragons Dogma 2* take the form of personal side quests associated with a given character.** These quests end with a brief romantic scene, which however does not have any major effects on the plot. Wilhelmina and Ulrika have personal romance quests.

2. After completing several main quests in Vernworth, you will meet Wilhelmina, the owner of the Rose Chateau borderlie brothel. **You'll receive a pass to enter the brothel, where you can use the services of the courtesans for 20,000 G. Purchasing the service results in a very short cutscene and has no gameplay benefits.**

Can you romance your own Pawn?

1. Since your main Pawn can be created from scratch and accompanies you throughout the game, **you may be wondering whether you can romance this character**.
2. **The main Pawn does not have a romance quest, meaning that you cannot romance them**. From players experience, sometimes your main Pawn may blush while talking to you - which usually means they have reached their maximum Affinity level - but this does not change the gameplay in any way and occurs very occasionally.

how to romance Ulrika?

One of the romance options in DD2 is Ulrika, the leader of the village of Melve. On this page of the guide we have described how to complete the quests related to her - Readvent of Calamity, Trouble on the Cape and home Is Where the hearth Is.

In *Dragon's Dogma 2*, there are a few short romance arcs involving certain characters important to the story that you can start and engage in. **One of the available romance options is Ulrika, the leader of Melve village, which is also a location visited early in the game.** Compared to Wilhelmina's, Ulrika's storyline is slightly longer and requires traveling between distant settlements, but it is also less complicated and easier to complete. **On this page of the guide, we show how to start a romance with Urlika and complete the quests that result from the affair**.

- how to start the romance?
- Readvent of Calamity
- Trouble on the Cape
- home Is Where the hearth Is

how to start the romance?

1. **To be able to start Ulrika's personal quests, you first need to proceed with the chain of the story quests received from Captain Brant in Wernworth.** After completing a sufficient number of tasks, Brant will ask you to visit Melve village once again. **This will start the Readvent of Calamity quest.**

   Warning - do not take part in the false Sovran's ceremony before completing the entirety of Ulrika's quest chain! The coronation event cancels many quests from Vermund, including romance/personal quests.

Readvent of Calamity

1. As you arrive in Melve, you'll see that a Drake is attacking the settlement. Fight the monster by focusing on attacking the shiny lumps on his body and keeping away from its maw to not be struck by his fiery breath. The entire population of Melve will help in the fight, so it shouldn't pose a serious problem - the beast will fly away once you've dealt enough damage to it.
2. **To continue with the chain, visit Melve from time to time (every few days).** You can also give Ulrika gifts to increase Affinity, but in our case this wasn't required. **During one of the visits to the village, go see Ulrika in her house - you'll encounter Martin, an official serving Queen Regent Disa who plans to accuse Ulrika of treason in order to take control of the village.** Continue by talking to Ulrika - you'll rest at her house today. **The next morning you will learn that Ulrika has escaped - you must find her.**

After fending off the monster, talk to Sigurd, a spear-wielding hooded warrior - this will unlock Mystic Spearhand vocation. If you miss him now, you can find him later in harve village.

Trouble on the Cape

This quest will start only if you've successfully completed Scaly Invaders, a different quest involving getting rid of Saurians from the village. If you haven't completed it yet, you need to do it now and return to the village later on to initiate Trouble on the Cape.

1. **You'll find Ulrlika in harve village, west from vernworth.** As you approach the quest location, you'll see Ulrlika arguing with the village leader. **Ulrika will disobey her orders and embark to Stormwind Cave to free a kidnapped villager. Join her.**
2. **Stormwind Cave is filled with hostile Saurians.** Luckily, you have Ulrika and a few other warriors at your side, so clearing the cave shouldn't be a problem. **As you reach the end of the cave, defeat the last group of Saurians to rescue the missing village and return to the cave entrance.** Ulrika will be proclaimed the new leader of the village. **Talk to her, and she will ask you to pass the news to Lennart. This will end this quest - you will receive 6,500 G and a Ferrystone.**
3. **Return to Melve and talk to Lennart, who can be found in Ulrika's house.** This will end Readvent of Calamity quest. **You will receive 4,500 G and Ring of Grit - a ring that reduces the stamina cost of shield blocking.**

home Is Where the hearth Is

You can make this quest considerably easier if, at the early stage of the game, you've helped Ian save his brother from wolves (brothers Brave and Timid quest). If you haven't completed this quest, before returning to Melve, make sure you have any 4 spare swords with you - for example, you can buy 4x Iron Sword at a blacksmith in Vernworth.

1. **To start this quest, you need to leave Melve and return after a few days** - in our case, we rode an Oxcart back to Vernworth, rested at the inn, and returned to Melve also by Oxcart. **As you arrive back to Melve, it will turn out that Queen Regent Disa's soldiers have taken over the village. To enter the village, you need to bribe the guard at the entrance gate with 5,000 G.** Go to Ulrika's house and talk to Lennart.

1. **Lennart will ask you to deliver 4 swords to him to arm the village inhabitants so they can rise to defeat the hostiles.** If you have previously helped Ian and Norbert, find them in the village and agree to help them. Ian will provoke the weapons warehouse guards to chase him, which will allow you to sneak into the building to steal the confiscated weapons. **Return to Lennart with the weapons.**
2. **A battle will ensue between the inhabitants and the occupying soldiers.** The guards are quite tough, but there are many allies with you. **With the soldiers defeated, the Melve inhabitants decide to relocate to Harve village. Follow them there.**

1. When you reach Harve village, talk to Ulrika. **If you have completed all mentioned quests, Ulrika will ask you to meet her at nighttime by the village docks.** Use a bench to change the time of the day and talk to Ulrika one last time. **This will end the quest and also conclude the romance. As a reward, you'll receive 12,000 G and Ring of Reassurance, an item that temporarily increases the defense of Pawns that have been helped get up.**

2. **After completing the quest, most of the NPCs from Melve will move to Harve village** - since this village is closer to the capital, interacting with them should be a bit more convenient now.

How to romance Wilhelmina?

One of the romance options in Dragons Dogma 2 is Wilhelmina, owner of the Rose Chateau borderlie. On this page of the guide we have described how to complete her personal quest, every Rose has Its Thorn.

In *Dragon's Dogma 2*, there are a few short romance arcs involving certain characters important to the story that you can start and engage in. **One of the available romance options is Wilhelmina, the owner of the Rose Chateau borderlie in Vernworth. On this page of our guide, we show how to romance this character and how to complete a personal quest for Wilhelmina - Rose has Its Thorn. We describe how to initiate the task and complete it successfully below.**

- How to start the romance?
- How to help Wilhelmina? (quest)

How to start the romance?

1. **To be able to start the personal quest for Wilhelmina, you first need to proceed with the chain of story quests received from Captain Brant.** The most important among them are **The Stolen Throne** (frequenting a masquerade ball) and **An Unsettling Encounter** (infiltrating the castle in search of secret documents). **You'll meet Wilhelmina during both of these quests, and the second meeting will result in her giving you an entry pass to the borderlie, which is a location you'll need to visit in order to start the personal quest.**

1. **next step is to increase Affinity with Wilhelmina**. You can find her on the upper floor of the borderlie - giving gifts and engaging in conversations should quickly increase her Affinity to the required level. In our case, a single conversation was enough. **When Wilhelmina's Affinity level reaches a sufficient level, you'll initiate a unique interaction.**

   Warning - do not take part in the false Sovran's ceremony before completing Wilhelmina's task! The coronation event cancels many quests from vermund, including romance/personal quests. before proceeding with the task, remember to also rest at the inn. This way, you'll be able to reload your save if the quest fails - which is possible, given that you cannot trust the quest markers entirely, while the best possible outcome of the quest requires a few non-obvious actions.

1. With the save made, go to the brothel. **Wilhelmina will not be in her chambers, and the employee standing next to the door will let you know that she is currently meeting with a client**. If Wilhemina is still in her room, leave vernworth and come back later. **Approach the small painting on the wall - you'll see a hole in the wall through which you can observe the meeting between Wilhelmina and Allard. In the next conversation, offer your help.** This will start the every Rose has Its Thorn quest.

how to help Wilhelmina? (quest)

1. **Wilhelmina is seeking revenge on Allard for the harm he caused, but she needs evidence. You have three days to obtain it** - make the quest a priority so that you don't run out of time.
2. **After you leave the borderlie, your Pawns will suggest the next step, which will be to visit Sven. You can find Sven in his chamber on the upper floor**

of the castle (provided you've completed his quest, The Ornate box). **Travel there immediately - before entering, make sure you have the full Marcher set (Marchers helm, Marchers Armor, and Marchers Cuisses) equipped as to not provoke the castle guards**. If you don't have such an armor, you can buy it from the armorsmith in Vernworth.

1. **Talk to Sven. he will suggest talking to his friend, Patrick, who can be only encountered at night**. Patrick will offer to help you - he will lead Allard away from his home, allowing you to infiltrate the estate. Once you agree to the plan, immediately go to Allard's house - it will be marked with a quest marker. **Go to the upper floor (bedroom) and examine the painting hanging on the wall. You'll find Murder Report, proving that Allard killed Wilhelmina's parents**.

    During the course of the quest, you may come across Allard and decide to warn him about Wilhelmina's plans. Don't do this - the quest will be cut short, resulting in a smaller reward and Queen Disa's helper surviving the affair.

1. You can already go present the evidence to Wilhelmina, but to get the best possible outcome, you need to do one more thing. **head to the Merchant Quarter, specifically to the house directly south of Clovis barberie. Inside, you'll find bribery Investigation Findings** - another piece of evidence that further proves that Allard engaged in bribery.

1. **With the obtained document, go to the inn and talk to Captain brant about the borderlie** (Tell me of the Myermecoleon). Present the bribery Investigation Findings and choose Search for More evidence dialogue option. Talk to him again and show him the Murder Report. now choose "I'll have any aid you can give" dialogue option. **This way you'll get brant and his help in the matter**.

1. **Travel to the borderlie and give Wilhelmina both documents - Murder Report and bribery Investigation Findings.** Agree to help her further, go to the neighboring room, lunge at Allard and pin him to the ground. **After the cut-scene, jump through the window to escape the guards - brant will be there to lead you to a safe place.** Follow him.

1. **Return to Wilhelmina's room the next night. This will end the quest and conclude the romance arc. As a reward, you will receive 8,500 G and Ring of benevolence** - a ring that regenerates health if the wielder suffered serious wounds. **Unfortunately, this will be your last interaction with Wilhelmina, as she disappears from the game once the quest is completed.**

Exploration

Is there an open world?

A title as high-profile as DD2 is stirring up interest in the community about the size of the world presented. On this page we will answer your questions about the game's open world.

Dragons Dogma 2 was announced as a massive RPG game full of various mechanics and activities. **The game's size also goes hand in hand with the size of the world it offers.** On this page, we answer whether you can move freely around the map in DD2, and we will also reveal additional information about the presented world.

- Open world

- What areas does the map consist of?

Open world

First, it is worth noting that **the world in *Dragons Dogma 2* is indeed open**. Players will be able to freely traverse vast terrains, discovering various treasures, secrets, and dangers along the way. Capcom's latest game is therefore consistent in this respect with the previous installment of the series.

Mechanics such as fast travel points and special camps that players can set up along the route will help them traverse the vast world.

What areas does the map consist of?

The map in *Dragons Dogma 2* **consists of 2 regions**:

1. **vermund** - a kingdom of people full of picturesque, green lands. The heart of the region is a vast, vibrant city, at the center of which is a fortified, royal residence. The sunlit vermund contrasts with the political intrigues unfolding behind the scenes.

1. **battahal** - the homeland of the beastern race, characterized by a much harsher climate. vast wastelands hide many relics of ancient civilizations, on the ruins of which a unique culture of animal-people was born. In this region, the accompanying Pawns are looked upon less favorably, while the faith of the inhabitants focuses around a mysterious flame surrounded by sacred reverence.

The world of DD2 is also inhabited by communities of elves, who, however, are not very willing to interact with the outside world. The language barrier also does not help in communication. however, it can be eliminated to some extent **thanks to the Pawn's specialization, who will translate this foreign language for you.**

What do the exclamation marks on the mini-map mean?

While playing DD2 you will often come across exclamation marks displayed on the minimap. On this page we have described what exclamation marks mean and how they appear.

The mini-map is one of the most useful elements of *Dragons Dogma 2*, significantly helping with orientation in the area. **The most common icon that appears on this map is an exclamation mark, which can indicate various places or interactive objects. This page of our guide describes what exclamation marks mean and when they appear on the mini-map.**

What are exclamation marks?

1. **exclamation marks are icons on the mini-map that indicate something worth noting**. It could be a Seeker Token, a chest, a group of enemies, a ladder, a document to read, and many others - you won't find out until you examine it. The exclamation mark in the picture above is for a ladder.

2. **The icon appears on the map when one of your Pawns notices an interesting object. That Pawn will say what they have noticed and an exclamation mark will appear on the mini-map.** It usually disappears after you interact with a given object. **It's worth paying attention to exclamation marks, as they may give you useful items.**

how to increase carrying capacity?

DD2 abounds with various pieces of equipment and items, the carrying of which can easily exhaust your character. On this page we will give you tips on how to increase your character's carrying capacity.

In *Dragons Dogma 2*, similarly to other RPGs, one of the core elements and mainstays of gameplay **is discovering, picking up, and collecting countless items**. however, in the case of the latest game from Capcom, mindless hoarding may quickly lead to inventory being full and the character becoming overencumbered. **On this page we explain the mechanics behind and show ways of increasing the hero's carrying capacity**.

- What are the factors behind carrying capacity?
- encumberance level
- how and where to find Golden Trove beetles?
- Increasing carrying capacity through leveling
- how to manage your inventory?

What are the factors behind carrying capacity?

Let's start with explaining the factors behind the overall carrying capacity of your Arisen. **Carrying capacity, similarly to, for example, Stamina, is one of the attributes describing the hero and is a result of what build you've chosen for your created hero**. Another important factor when wanting to increase carrying capacity is the weight of a character. **The more weighty your hero is, the more he can carry**. So if you plan to have expanded carrying capabilities, a good idea would be to create a bulky hero.

You can read more about character creation and factors influencing the hero on Character Creator page of our guide.

encumberance level

The current encumbrance level is also reflected by a special indicator. **Depending on your current encumbrance level, your hero will be more or less affected by a special status** that affects properties such as:

1. **Stamina consumption and regeneration;**
2. **Movement speed;**
3. **Climbing.**

The general rule, however, is that **the lighter the inventory, the better your Arisen handles demanding physical actions**. That's why it's very important to skillfully manage equipment and distribute items across team members.

how and where to find Golden Trove beetles?

A direct way of increasing carrying capacity of your hero is finding and eating a bug called Golden Trove beetle. You'll find them to be common in wilderness, often perching on tree trunks. They additionally emit a delicate golden glow making them easy to spot, especially at nighttime. **After picking up the beetle, you can eat it, which will increase your character's carrying capacity by 0.15 kg.**

This bonus may seem small, but after eating a sufficient number of these insects, your carrying capacity will improve noticeably. **Your main Pawn can also consume these insects.**

Increasing carrying capacity through leveling

Throughout the game, your carrying capacity will naturally increase as you level up. The extent to which your carrying capacity will increase is determined by the protagonist's build and stature. however, it can be safely assumed that a high-level Arisen will be much better at carrying many things at once than a low level one.

how to manage your inventory?

To avoid the consequences of overencumbrance, a crucial element of DD2 will be proper inventory management. **The matter only requires small inputs made from time to time - dividing items between team members and removing or selling unneeded junk on a regular basis.** If your hero is of small build and cannot carry much, **a good idea would be to create or recruit Pawns of large stature that will help carry the heaviest items.**

The services of a Logistician Pawn will also be useful. **This type of companion will automatically distribute the found items among everyone in the team, and will also craft items based on ingredients he carries in his inventory regularly.**

Is there fast travel?

The world of DD2 is vast and full of dangers that could be bypassed by fast travel. On this page of our guide we have described if there is a fast travel in the game. *Dragons Dogma 2* is set in a huge world full of dangers, and slow traversing of the map is in itself a large part of the experience. This means that fast travel is often a luxury or a convenience that you won't always be able to afford or freely use. **On this page of our guide, we explain whether there is fast travel in the game and how safe is to travel between locations.**

- Is there fast travel in the game?
- Oxcart
- Portcrystals and Ferrystones

Is there fast travel in the game?

1. **Yes, there is something in the game that can be called fast travel, but it slightly differs from the mechanics of a similar name encountered in modern games.** *Dragon's Dogma 2* places great emphasis on immersion - exploration is how you come across and begin various adventures and events, making fast travel more of a gimmick and a rare occurrence that you won't enjoy often. **There are two main methods of fast travel, both of which we describe below.**

Oxcart

1. **The most common and cheap method of traveling are Oxcarts - ox-drawn carts led around main routes between settlements.** You can come across them mid-ride in the wild, or in settlements, where they are found at Oxcart Stations.

There are also special columns at the stations - interacting with them will fast-forward the time until the arrival of the next Oxcart automatically.

2. **To board an Oxcart, you need to sit on a red scarf on one of the seats. The driver will let you know to which settlement Oxcart is heading and will ask for a fee (100 G).** You can then stay awake for the entire journey or take a nap - the second option will fast-forward the trip, with you awaking already at the destination. **Traveling via Oxcarts causes time to pass, so keep that in mind if you've accepted any time-limited quests.**

1. **When traveling in a Oxcart, you can be attacked by enemies - including bosses.** The journey will be interrupted, and you, along with the wagon escort, will have to get rid of the enemies. After defeating them, you can resume your ride by getting back in the Oxcart.

2. **There is a possibility that Oxcart will be destroyed during an ambush.** You can see this in the screenshot above - during the fight with an ogre who attacked the travelers, the monster jumped on the wagon, tipping it over and killing the oxen pulling it. **If the Oxcart is destroyed, you will not be able to continue your journey, instead having to proceed on foot for the rest of the way - additionally, you won't get your money back.** Try to distract enemies from the Oxcart during ambushes to avoid its destruction.

Portcrystals and Ferrystones

1. **The second means of fast travel is faster, more convenient, safer, but also much more expensive.** Occasionally, in some larger cities, you will come across Portcrystals stations used for fast travel. **Once you interact with one, it will be added to your list of destinations.** They are a rather rare occurrence, as many

lesser settlements won't have one, but **at some point in the game you will have the option to place your own Portcrystals in the locations of your choice.**

2. **To use Portcrystals you need Ferrystones.** These are consumables that can be found during exploration or bought at a store. **After consuming a Ferrystone to perform a travel, you lose it irrevocably. Travelling with them is instant and doesn't cause passage of time.**

3. The disadvantage of this method is it price and inaccessibility. Ferrystone is a rare and expensive item that cannot be obtained commonly. even if you find a store that sells it (e.g. **Philbert's Sundries in Vernworth**), you must be able to afford them. **One Ferrystone costs 10,000 G**, which is a very considerable sum, especially at the beginning of the game. **For this reason, this method of fast travel only becomes viable later in the game.**

how to find the elf village?

In one of the forests of Dragons Dogma 2 lies Sacred Arbor, a hidden village of elves. On this page of the guide we have described how to find it, what may stand in your way, what interesting things you will find in the village and how to understand the elven language.

The elven village of Sacred Arbor is a completely optional location that is not required to be visited to complete the game. however, it is worth your attention, especially if you play as the Archer vocation or plan to develop this class. **On this page of the guide, we have described where to find the Sacred Arbor, what enemies may stand in your way, what you can find inside the village and how to understand the elvish language.**

- Where is Sacred Arbor?
- What can be found in Sacred Arbor?
- how to learn the elvish language?

Where is Sacred Arbor?

1. **Sacred Arbor is located west of the Melve village.** Since both settlements are separated from each other by water, you will have to get there by traveling from Vernworth.

2. **You can be guided to the settlement by the elf Glyndwr, who knows the human language and can be found in the market square in Vernworth.** To start his quest, you must give him any human-made bow - you can buy one from the armory nearby. **Completing his quest is worth it, especially if you play as an Archer, because his father Taliesin will then become an Archer class Meister and teach you the special skill Heavenly Shot, which deals massive damage in exchange for absorbing all of your stamina.**

1. **In the forest surrounding the settlement, you may encounter powerful enemies, e.g. Chimeras and Golems.** Go there when you are sure you can handle them - **we recommend that you be at least level 20, or maybe even a few levels higher.**

What can be found in Sacred Arbor?

1. **Apart from the previously mentioned Heavenly Shot ability, the main attraction of the Sacred Arbor is the Grisha's Armory store.** You will find there a lot of useful equipment, mainly for Archer, Mage and Sorcerer classes. **They also sell weapons for the secret Magick Archer class, which you can unlock in the final stage of the game.**

2. The second available store, eldart's Apothecary, sells elixirs that cure almost all status effects in the game.

how to learn the elvish language?

1. **elves speak a different language from humans, which means you are unable to communicate with them**. The subtitles under the dialogues and the dialogue options are written in elvish - you can choose dialogue options, but you won't know what they mean.
2. **Although your main character cannot learn elvish, they can get a translator in the form of any Pawn with the Woodland Wordsmith specialization**. As long as such a Pawn is in your party, the dialogues will be automatically written in a language understandable to you. **Recruit a Pawn with this specialization before heading to the Sacred Arbor** - Riftstones allow you to sort Pawns according to their specialization.

Mechanics and Collectibles

Is there multiplayer?

DD2 is set in a huge, beautiful world that many players would like to explore with friends. On this page of the guide we describe whether the game includes multiplayer or co-op mode.

The world of *Dragon's Dogma 2* is huge, full of adventures to find, unexpected events and dangerous enemies. For this reason, many players may wonder if there is an option to explore this land alongside friends. **On this page of our guide, we explain whether *Dragon's Dogma 2* includes co-op or other multiplayer modes.**

Multiplayer in Dragons Dogma 2

Unfortunately, *Dragon's Dogma 2* does not feature any multiplayer mode. You will only be able to play alone - although the Pawns system, i.e. companions controlled by advanced artificial intelligence, recreates, to some extent, the experience that could come from a multiplayer game.

The lack of multiplayer, however, does not mean that *Dragon's Dogma 2* is completely devoid of online functions. This is where the above-mentioned Pawns come into play again, as players can create them themselves and then share them with the community. This means that although you can't finish the game together with a friend, an ally created by them can keep you company.

how to cast spells?

Several vocations available in DD2 involve the use of spells during combat. On this page, we will explain to you the basics related to enchantment, which will help you get used to it when you first encounter a magical character class.

When choosing a starting vocation, many of you may notice the Mage class - **a ruler of arcane knowledge who fights with a staff, strikes enemies with lightning and heals their companions with healing spells.** On this page, we will present you with the most important information related to casting spells and **we will give you a handful of tips that will make it easier for you to start your adventure as a Mage.**

- how to cast spells?
- how to speed up spell casting?

how to cast spells?

After selecting the Mage vocation in character creator, **you will be get your first staff in the tutorial**. This type of weapon has a basic attack, **Focused bolt, which sends a magic projectile towards the opponent**. The energy orb basically flies instantly, does not consume any resources, and has a decent range, which allows the Mage to flood the opponents with a hail of projectiles between casting more powerful spells.

In addition to Focused bolt, the Mage also has access to the basic healing spell - **Anodyne. After casting it, a semicircular sphere appears around a hero, regenerating part of their health**. both the protagonist and the companions within the spell's range.

by holding the appropriate button, you gain access to more advanced skills, or the spells that interest you the most. The basic offensive spell is the fiery **Flagration**. After selecting it, the Mage will begin an incantation (the enchantment process), **during which their speed drops significantly and they become defenseless**. That's why it's so important to position yourself correctly on the battlefield and rely on the companions who are defending you. **If the incantation is interrupted by an enemy, you will need to start it over again**.

If you are close enough to the enemy, **a circle will appear around them during the incantation to help you aim**. You can hold the spell for a while and release it at a convenient moment. This pattern is the same in the case of later, more powerful spells.

be aware, however, that **many late-game spells may have significantly increased incantation times**. This will be particularly noticeable if you decide to change your vocation to Sorcerer, whose more powerful attacks are offset by increased preparation time.

how to speed up spell casting?

however, there is a fairly simple way to speed up the incantation time of individual spells. After unlocking the development of vocations at an early stage of the game, in the Mage's basic abilities tab you will find the **Quickspell** perk. **It allows you to significantly speed up the spell casting time at the expense of your stamina.** While casting a spell, hold down the appropriate button. Used at a crucial moment, it allows for an instant casting of a spell. however, pay attention to the health bar, because if your weakened character is surrounded by enemies, you can easily die.

how to save the game?

DD2 offers several options for saving the game state. On this page, we will tell you how they differ and which one to use at what point.

In *Dragons Dogma 2*, players can save their progress in several ways. **each of the available forms of saving one's progress is treated by the game in a slightly different way.** before starting the game, it is important to familiarize yourself with all available options to avoid unpleasant surprises such as accidentally overwriting one's progress. **This page explains all the available variants.**

- Manual saves
- Saving at the tavern
- Loading the game after death

- Can I start a new game?

Manual saves

The basic way to save the game is to use the appropriate option from the menu. At almost any point in the game, you can navigate to the pause screen, where you can choose the last option - "System". **In the "Save" tab you can decide whether you want to save the game and continue playing, save and exit to the main menu, or exit the game without saving.**

To resume the game, **select the "Load from Last Save" option on the title screen**. DD2 will get you to the place where you last created a manual save. DD2 also saves the game automatically. During exploration, the game will occasionally make an additional save for you, which will replace the last manual save. however, our experience shows that this automated system works quite selectively, and it is good practice to make a manual save from time to time on your own.

Saving at the tavern

An alternative way to save the game is to rest in a tavern. If you decide to use the services of a similar establishment (marked with a bed icon on the map), **in addition to regenerating your health and stamina, the game will remember your location, to which you will be able to return in the future.**

To load the game in the last inn you visited, **select the "Load form Last Inn Rest" option from the main menu. This option will overwrite any manual save made** after resting. It will be especially useful in situations where your manual save is in a rather unfortunate place, and you would like to repeat a certain section of the game. For this reason, **it is a very good idea to visit taverns from time to time, which will create a series of "spare" save files for you.**

What is very important - **ReSTInG In CAMPS DOeS nOT COUnT AS ReST AT An Inn!** Although spending the night by the fire will allow your party to regenerate, it will not create an additional save file. **The option to load the game from an inn will always place you in the last tavern where you spent the night.**

Loading the game after death

If your character dies, the game will give you the option to load the game from the last save point. **however, this option comes with a penalty in the form of lowering your maximum health level.** This debuff will certainly not help you when trying to complete a difficult sequence again, and **regaining full health will require you to rest at an inn or camp.**

The second option is to load the game from the last inn where you rested. **This option does not come with any additional penalty.** So this is another reason why it is so important to regularly visit and save the game at the inns scattered around the map.

Can I start a new game?

Unfortunately, at the moment *Dragons Dogma 2* **does not support multiple saves** - you can only start one game, which cannot be deleted later. **To start a new playthrough from scratch, you must either complete the game and start new Game Plus, or delete all save files** (which means you will not be able to go back to your original playthrough). **Capcom has promised to introduce the possibility of starting a new game in the unspecified future**, but for now deleting save files is the only option.

Deleting save files on PC consists of two steps. First, you need to disable Steam Cloud - to do this, go to the Steam platform and right-click on *Dragon's Dogma 2* in your game library. Click "Properties" and uncheck the option "Keep games saves in the Steam Cloud".

Then you need to go into the game files and manually delete your save file. Go to Local disk (C):/Program Files (x86)/Steam/userdata. next, go to the folder indicating your Steam profile (it is saved as several numbers in a row, there will be as many folders as you have profiles registered on your computer). now you need to find the save files for *Dragons Dogma 2* - they are hidden in the 2054970 folder. **Lastly, go to the remote folder and delete the win64_save folder. This will permanently delete your save files and allow you to start the game completely from the beginning.**

What are Wakestones used for?

Wakestone are rare and extremely valuable items that you will encounter in DD2. On this page of the guide we have explained how to acquire them and their uses. One of the rarest items in *Dragons Dogma 2* are Wakestones - magical stones with extraordinary power. **They can get you out of many situations, but you must use them wisely. On this page of the guide, we explain how to obtain Wakestones, what they are for and under what circumstances you should use them. We also described what morgues, buildings strongly associated with Wakestones, are used for.**

- What are Wakestones used for?
- What is a morgue used for?
- how to obtain Wakestones?

What are Wakestones used for?

1. Wakestones have two main uses, although they are based on the same thing - **they enable you to bring a dead character back to life once**. Its first use is, as you might guess, resurrecting the playable character after death. If you have at least one Wakestone in your inventory and your main character dies, the game will ask you if you want to use the Wakestone to bring them back to life.

2. Refusal is the end of the game - you can load the previous save or go back to the previous inn. **If you agree, you will lose the Wakestone and your character will come back from the dead, enabling you to continue the adventure**. Since Wakestones are rare, it is best to consume them during difficult battles if you died while being close to victory.

What is a morgue used for?

1. **The second main use of Wakestone is to resurrect dead nPCs**. Independent characters can die as a result of failed quests, monster attacks, etc. Their bodies are being transferred to the nearest morgue in the nearest settlement. **If you go to the mortuary and find a dead nPC there, you can use a Wakestone to bring them back to life**. but you have to hurry - **the body will only stay in the mortuary for a few days. After a short time, they will be buried, which equals the permanent death of the nPC**.

how to obtain Wakestones?

1. The process of acquiring Wakestone is somewhat more complicated than with other items. **To craft a Wakestone, you must first obtain three Wakestone Shards**. You will find these items by completing optional quests or exploring the

world and opening the chests you encounter. **When you collect three Wakestone Shards, they will automatically combine in your inventory into one Wakestone**.

What are the uses of Seeker Tokens?

Seekers Tokens are the most common find in DD2. These tokens can be exchanged for various rewards at guild headquarters. On this page we've listed all the rewards you can earn with Seekers Tokens.

In the world of *Dragons Dogma 2*, **the most common type of collectible** are Seeker Tokens, **small badges that can be exchanged for valuable rewards in Guild headquarters. each collectible of this type is numbered, and there are a total of 220 of them**, hidden in various locations across the world of the game, be it settlements, enemy camps, or ruins. **They remain hidden until you get close to one** - when you approach a suitable area, an exclamation mark icon will appear on the minimap marking the exact location of the collectible. **On this page of our guide, we list all rewards that can be received from donating Seeker Tokens, and where to find them.**

Rewards for Seeker Tokens

You can receive rewards for Seeker Tokens by exchanging them in Guild headquarters, which are found in every major city. To get new rewards, you need to cross a certain Token threshold. The available rewards are:

1 Token - Ferrystone (a stone allowing one fast travel per item),

5 Tokens - Ring of vehemence (a ring slightly increasing the chance of staggering and knocking down enemies with your attacks),

15 Tokens - Ring of Triumph (a ring slightly increasing maximum health, stamina, and carrying capacity),

30 Tokens - Dowsing Spikes (a set of Daggers that glow when close to a treasure),

50 Tokens - Twilight Star (a Circlet increasing resistance to status effects),

70 Tokens - Ring of Profusion (Ring, moderately increases carrying capacity),

90 Tokens - Champion's Mantle (Cloak, increasing electricity resistance),

120 Tokens - eternal bond (a ring having a certain unspecified effect on companions),

150 Tokens - Charming Corset (an armour item of excellent statistics),

180 Tokens - Legion's Might (Staff, when equipped by a Pawn makes him able to rise after being knocked down).

220 Tokens - Ring of endeavor (Ring, slightly increases Discipline points gain from defeating enemies).

Is there a day and night cycle?

DD2 offers quite advanced time lapse mechanics affecting various elements of the game world. On this page we will give you the most important information about it. While playing **Dragons Dogma 2, you'll be affected by the passage of time in a multitude of ways.** Ingredients left for too long in the inventory will go bad and lose their properties, time-limited tasks will force you to carefully plan your activities and order of them, while destroyed structures will get rebuilt after a few days. **however, the most obvious indicator of the passage of time is the daily cycle.** On this page of our guide, we provide the most important information regarding the passage of time and the day and night cycle, which should help you prepare well for the challenges ahead.

- What are the dangers of travelling at night?
- Daily cycle of nPCs
- how to speed up the passage of time?

What are the dangers of travelling at night?

When traveling at night, you must bear in mind that **your effective sight range may be reduced greatly**. The lack of lights along beaten paths will require your team to use lanterns to light the way forward. For this reason, **it is always worth having a supply of lantern oil brought with you**.
If your Arisen lights up his lantern, the rest of the team will follow his lead and also light up their lights.

When traveling at night, you can also expect increased monster activity. You may encounter exclusive, more dangerous monsters such as specters and undead who normally avoid daylight. **When it comes to common enemies, fighting them can be more troublesome because of the darkness surrounding the area.** When in dangerous situations, it is recommended to stay alert, proceed slowly, and rely on sounds to detect incoming threats.

If you want to avoid the risks associated with traveling at night, you can choose to spend the night at a campsite. The light of a campfire will allow you to wait out until morning, but you're not fully safe. **If you do not clear the area of potential threats in advance, your sleep may be disturbed by a sudden attack by goblins, wolves or the undead**. In that case, you will have to neutralize the threat before you can go back to sleep.

Daily cycle of nPCs

When attempting to interact with characters inhabiting the world of DD2, **keep in mind that each has his unique daily cycle**. For example, if you are looking for a specific nPC, it may happen that you won't find him at his home during the day and instead, he will complete errands in the city streets. **Some nPCs only frequent certain locations at certain times**, so it's recommended to plan your visit and check which hour will be the best for a visit in advance.

how to speed up the passage of time?

To quickly speed up the passage of time, you can e.g. establish a camp and sleep, in the manner same as we described above. **Inns are venues offering similar services**, and when staying in them, you can decide for how long the team should rest, e.g until the next morning or evening. Additional option is to interact **with special locations marked with red cloth**. This way you can instantly "fast-forward" time to the chosen time of the day. You will find such locations in city streets and same option is offered by carts used to travel between settlements.

What items can be safely sold?

Traveling through the vast world of DD2, you will come to find a mass of various items. On this page we will suggest to you which of them are worth selling.
Dragons Dogma 2, like many other open-world RPGs, leaves the player with a wide range of items and ingredients such as weapons, armor items, food or valuables to find and put in the inventory during our adventures. **however, you cannot hoard**

everything - to properly manage your inventory, avoid cluttering and a mobility hit, selling unneeded and surplus items is recommended. On this page, we explain what items can be safely traded off without the risk of losing something valuable or useful.

- Old equipment
- Decaying ingredients and excess potions
- beware of selling plot items!

Old equipment

As you progress in the game, you will find new equipment that may be better than what you and your team have currently equipped. The first step to avoiding overencumbrance which can be done on the spot is handing down your old weapons and armor items to one of your Pawns. **however, if the old equipment is of no use to anyone in your team, you can always sell it**. You will gain some cash from this, and also free up a lot of space in your inventory.

The ideal place to sell equipment will be armor merchants. **Merchants specializing in this field are marked with a helmet icon, while weapon salesmen are indicated with a sword icon.**

Decaying ingredients and excess potions

In DD2, an innovative mechanic has been introduced in which ingredients such as fruit or meat will go bad if left in the inventory for too long. **The best way of avoiding this is mixing less durable ingredients into various potions and dishes on a regular basis.**

If wares created this way start to take too much space in the inventory, you can sell them at wandering merchants or in cities. **Apothecaries specializing in potions and herbs are marked with a vial icon on the map**. Although individual items of this type do not fetch a high price, selling them is a much better idea than leaving them in the inventory to rot.

Although vendors in DD2 have their narrow specializations and offer only chosen types of products, when it comes to selling, they are much less picky. Most of them will happily buy almost anything from you, even if the product does not match their profession.

Beware of selling plot items!

Dragons Dogma 2 **does not in any way prohibits or stays your hand when attempting to sell important story items**. For this reason, you must be especially careful what you put up for sale at merchants, as not to accidentally get rid of an important quest item, without which you may not be able to successfully complete a given task.

Why does my maximum health decrease over time?

Declining maximum health is one of the key mechanics of DD2. On this page of the guide, we have explained why the maximum health of your character and pawns is declining and whether it can be remedied.

In *Dragons Dogma 2*, constant plunging into the heat of action and battle and taking wounds can have an unpleasant effect in the form of maximum health capacity taking a hit and being gradually lowered. This effect can really take its toll on the gameplay, often forcing you to retreat from a promising excursion and forsaking your progress, which can be frustrating as well as problematic. **On this page of our guide, we explain the reasons behind lowered health capacity and how to counter it.**

- Why does my maximum health decrease over time?
- how to counter the health loss?

Why does my maximum health decrease over time?

1. even if it may seem that way, the diminishing maximum health was envisioned by the developers as an immersion-creating mechanic rather than just being a bug. It is called by the game as Loss effect. When you take damage during battles, a portion of the damage received affects your maximum health - **you may consider this as an attempt to make wounds more permanent and lasting and affecting the hero.** The effect can accumulate very fast if you've received a series of hits one after another cause of an unlucky streak, making further battles much harder because of the lowered effectiveness of your hero.

2. **The Loss effect also comes into play when you die and decide to load the latest save game at the game over screen.** This means that at each next attempt at a given battle is harder than the previous one, as with each try you have less health which means chances of dying are increased.

how to counter the health loss?

1. **Unfortunately, there isn't a simple method (potion/spell) to remedy the Loss effect**, as it is treated as a key game mechanic that is supposed to build immersion. **The longer you're in the wild and more skirmishes you weather, the weaker you become.**

2. While there is no remedy for this you can craft, you can counter the health loss by resting at an inn (requires a fee) or at a bonfire (requires a

camping kit). Such a longer rest will bring the maximum health of both the Arisen and his team to its original capacity. As can be easily understood, this mechanic encourages regular resting and adventuring in moderation.

3. **Another option here is choosing the Load from last Inn Rest option in the game over screen - choosing this option will load a save right after resting when your health is at full capacity. however be careful with choosing that option, as it will revert the entire progress you've made from the last inn rest.** Resting at bonfires isn't treated by the game as a rest in an inn and doesn't create a separate save state - this means that Load from Last Inn Rest will ignore all rests you've made at bonfires.

how to unlock Dwarven Smithing?

Dwarvem Smithing is a special type of equipment upgrade in DD2. On this page we will show you where to start and how to complete the Put a Spring in Thy Step quest that will allow you to unlock them.

Dwarven Smithing is one of the equipment upgrade styles available in the game. A weapon enhanced in this way is characterized by greater knockdown power, while improved armor will allow you to take more damage without making your hero lose balance. **Unlocking Dwarven Smithing will require completing a specific side quest in the battahl region.** On this page we will explain how to do this.

- how to start the Put a Spring in Thy Step quest?
- how to get to Geyser hamlet with Gautstafr?
- how to improve equipment with Dwarven Smithing?

how to start the Put a Spring in Thy Step quest?

To start the quest that will give you the opportunity to use Dwarven Smithing, **you must go to the western edge of Volcanic Island - located south of Battahl.** You will get there by going through the Spellseal Door in Bakbattahl. **To open it, however, you will have to progress to A new Godsway main quest.** This is a stage in the second half of the game, after the coronation of the false Arisen, a few quests after arriving and starting the storyline in the capital of Battahl.

An alternative is to take the road south of the capital and cross Drabnir's Grotto, which connects Battahl with the Volcanic Island. This road is teeming with enemies (bandits, knackers, harpies), and in the cave itself, you must watch out for groups of hobgoblins and an armored Cyclops guarding the exit. **however, if you manage to get out on the other side, you will find yourself right next to the starting location of the quest you are looking for.**

While walking along the main road in the western part of the island, you encounter a bent old man named Gautstafr. Talk to him. Complaining about back pain, **he will ask you to find 3 healing plants.** You can look for:

1. **Goldthistle;**
2. **Pitywort;**
3. **Morningtide;**
4. **Syrupwort Leaf.**

It's very possible that at this stage of the game you will have the appropriate amount of these plants in your inventory. **If not, check your Pawns' inventory or look around the area.** Commonly occurring ingredients should not be too difficult to find.

After you give Gautstafr the ingredients, he will thank you and invite you to his house. The active task marker on the map will help you get there. **The cottage is located by the sea, not far north from the place of the first meeting.**

Upon arrival, you will witness a brief argument between the old man and his elven beloved - Cliodhna. During the conversation, Gautstafr will start complaining about his aching back again. **Suggest to him an escort to the Geyser hamlet healing springs. The man will agree to your offer and the task objective will be updated.**

how to get to Geyser hamlet with Gautstafr?

Leave Gautstafr's hut and follow the road west. The man doesn't move too fast so every now and then stop so he can catch up. If you run too fast, the old man will stop you and ask to slow down.
If Gautstafr's speed irritates you, you can try to carry him. however, remember that from time to time you will have to put him on the ground to deal with dangers on the route.

There are two paths leading to Volcanic Island Camp:
1. **northern** - shorter, closer to the ocean, leading through caves;
2. **Southern** - longer, most of the time in open space.

From our experience, there is a high probability of encountering a large opponent (i.e., one with a separate health bar at the top of the screen) on both paths. In the case of coastal caves, it was a Minotaur, while in the south - a Cyclops and a Golem. On both roads we also encountered a Griffin and numerous groups of hobgoblins.

The artificial intelligence controlling Gautstafr handles avoiding trouble during combat quite well, and the old man himself is quite resistant to damage. **Therefore, you should not worry about his safety even during more fierce battles.**

After reaching the settlement, head towards the wooden scaffolding in its center. Go all the way up, and then through the small tunnel. You will reach the healing springs hidden among volcanic rocks.

Upon entering the bathhouse building, Gautstafr will thank you for your help and immediately head to the hot springs. **his beloved Cliodhna will also appear and will give you 23,000 gold and Laurel Circlet as a reward.** The archery master also unlocks the Magick-Archer vocation for you, and offer a scroll teaching the Spellbow's Paradox master skill for this class.

how to improve equipment with Dwarven Smithing?

After completing the Put a Spring in Thy Step quest, you can return to Gautstafr's house, which from now on will function as a weapon store. **by selecting the "enhance equipment" option, you will be able to use Dwarven Smithing.**

The Dwarven Smithing style is characterized by the following properties:

1. **The weapon has a greater piercing power, which can knock the enemy off balance;**
2. **Armors increase your resistance to being knocked off balance.**

The Dwarven upgrade will therefore work well for classes that fight with melee weapons, such as **Fighter** or **Warrior**.

To upgrade your weapon or armor, select the item you are interested in from the list on the left. The middle table will show you **what ingredients you will need to provide and how much you will have to pay for the upgrade**. every item has 3 slots for upgrades and it's up to you whether you decide to invest all of them in one style (such as the Dwarven Smithing mentioned here), or maybe combine several different ones. **The decision will be made easier for you by the table on the right side, where you can see how the item's statistics will change after the upgrade.**

What is Dragonsplague?

Dragonsplague is one of the most subtle, yet most dangerous mechanics in the entire DD2 game. On this page of the guide, we explain what it is, how to detect it and the consequences of ignoring it.

While playing *Dragons Dogma 2*, sooner or later your pawns will start talking about Dragonsplague - a mysterious disease that only Pawns can suffer from. Although at first this dialogue may seem like just world building, Dragonsplague does exist - and even you, as the main characters, are not safe. **On this page of the guide, we have described what Dragonsplague is, what causes the disease, how to detect it, how to get rid of it and what are the consequences of ignoring or overlooking it.**

- What is Dragonsplague and how can one catch it?
- What does Dragonsplague lead to?
- how to cure Dragonsplague?

What is Dragonsplague and how can one catch it?

1. **Dragonsplague is a disease that affects the minds of Pawns.** As its name suggests, the source is dragons. **There are two ways to catch Dragonsplague. The first is getting infected by another, already sick Pawn. The second is infection by dragon-like enemies, such as Drake** - infection is caused by a grapple attack that these dangerous bosses use. **Some Pawns you hired online may also already have Dragonsplague.**

2. Dragonsplague develops in the infected Pawn for several days and its symptoms increase over time and become more noticeable. **The infected Pawn becomes more powerful, but also rebellious. They will start refusing to obey orders, talk back or even insult the main character. Standing still, they may start holding their head and shaking with pain. The most obvious symptom is red eyes that develop over time.**

3. **Your first encounter with Dragonsplague displays a tutorial that will inform you about this disease.** Thanks to this, you will be sure that one of your Pawns is sick, but only this one time - **you will have to diagnose the next cases on your own.**

What does Dragonsplague lead to?

1. **The consequences of overlooking or ignoring Dragonsplague are enormous.** If you have spent a few days with a sick Pawn, allowing the disease to reach a critical stage, your next rest at home or at an inn will bring an unpleasant surprise. **The sick Pawn will undergo a transformation and return to where it came from, triggering an explosion of evil magic.**

2. When you wake up, the infected Pawn will no longer be in your party. **Moreover, almost all nPCs in a given settlement will be killed. Regular**

NPCs, shopkeepers, and even key quest characters, such as Captain Brant, can become a victim. Their death will also prevent you from completing the quests they are associated with. Although characters can be resurrected using Wakestone, there will be too many casualties to resurrect everyone. **The only way to reverse the massacre is to use the very rare eternal Wakestone, which most players will never even encounter.**

3. **Although the main plot can be completed despite the death of important NPCs, you will be left without any clues** and will have to blindly look for the next.

How to cure Dragonsplague?

1. **There are two ways to get rid of Dragonsplague and neither is pleasant. The first is to infect another Pawn** - the infecting Pawn will then be cured. This method can work against you because **a sick Pawn can easily infect your main Pawn**.

2. **The second, and at the same time the only practical way, is to get rid of the sick Pawn. The death of a Pawn destroys the disease** - you can then summon them back at a Riftstone. **The easiest way to eliminate a Pawn is by picking them up and dropping them from a height or throw into deep water.**

3. **You can also dismiss the sick Pawn at a Riftstone** - but this will endanger other players if you play online.

4. To effectively protect yourself from Dragonsplague, you must be very careful. **Pay attention to what your Pawns say and how they behave, look out for symptoms and don't hesitate to kill a Pawn if you suspect the disease** - you can always summon them again using Riftstone. **When hiring Pawns from other players, pay attention to their appearance, watch their eyes and listen to how they introduce themselves.**

5. **If Dragonsplague worries you, you can reduce the chances of it happening by playing offline.** None of the Pawns created by Capcom are affected

by Dragonsplague, so you won't be exposed to it by hiring them - **the only way to get it will then be one specific attack from the Drakes**.

Printed in Great Britain
by Amazon